*Christian Missions and
the Judgment of God*

Christian Missions and the Judgment of God

DAVID MACDONALD PATON

Second Edition

Edited with short biography by
DAVID M. M. PATON

With an Introduction by
REV. BOB WHYTE

Foreword by
BISHOP K. H. TING
President of the China Christian Council

WILLIAM B. EERDMANS PUBLISHING COMPANY
GRAND RAPIDS, MICHIGAN / CAMBRIDGE, U.K.

© 1996 Wm. B. Eerdmans Publishing Co.
255 Jefferson Ave. S.E., Grand Rapids, Michigan 49503 /
P.O. Box 163, Cambridge CB3 9PU U.K.

Printed in the United States of America

01 00 99 98 97 96   7 6 5 4 3 2 1

Library of Congress Cataloging-in-Publication Data

Paton, David Macdonald.
    Christian missions and the judgment of God /
David Macdonald Paton; edited with short biography
by David M. M. Paton; with an introduction
by Bob Whyte; foreword by K. H. Ting. — 2nd ed.
    p.   cm.
    Includes bibliographical references.
    ISBN 0-8028-4087-6 (alk. paper)
    1. Missions. 2. Paton, David Macdonald.
I. Paton, David M. M. II. Title.
BV2061.P37 1996
    266 — dc20   96-9150
                                        CIP

For

A. G. P.
A. W. P.
M. J. W.

And to the Memory of

David Macdonald Paton, 1913-1992

Contents

Foreword

In the year 1953, there appeared a book of only seventy-nine pages, published by the SCM Press in London, which brought forth much anger and outcry that such a naughty work should have surfaced. It was indeed an "untimely" book, an almost ruthless self-criticism of missionary work in general and in China in particular, at a time when China missionaries had just had their exodus en bloc and what was left of their work was in great disarray. The very title of the book — *Christian Missions and the Judgment of God* — sounded outrageous, since the judgment of God could only be rightly reserved for those to whom mission went, and not for the missions themselves.

Yet in the last forty years there has been a growing demand for the book, the call for its reprint is widespread, and there is general international appreciation for what it has meant for the emergence of a new missiology.

There is a Chinese adage that says, "Faithful words do not easily enter one's ears, just as good medication tastes bitter in one's mouth." Granted that there may be overstatements, *Christian Missions and the Judgment of God* is not anti-missionary. It is a book of prophetic vision, which came just in time for initiating a reevaluation of the whole cause. It offered some bitter medicine at a time when so many Christians in China and outside saw no hope. "New occasions teach new duties, Time makes ancient good uncouth," as the hymn says. The author quotes Chancellor T. R. Milford so aptly: "Christians must learn again what Christians have always known, how to live without immediate hopes in the world."

David Paton belongs to the school of missiological thinking with Roland Allen at its head. The experience of the church in China in the last forty years bears out the great truth in the teaching of both of them that the planting of churches that can survive is a more urgent task than just seeking to increase the number of converts. It outlasts the departure of preachers, be they foreign or national. To make the church in China self-governing, self-supporting, and self-propagating, and on the top of that, to govern ourselves well, to support ourselves well, and to do the work of Christian propagation well — that is church planting.

David Paton is a gift of God to the worldwide church in just such a time as this.

K. H. Ting
Nanjing, China

Preface to the Second Edition

The idea for a second edition of my father's book arose out of conversations with several of his old friends at the memorial service in Gloucester. Some felt that he had not received due recognition from the church in his lifetime for his unusual and radical service; all felt that *Christian Missions and the Judgment of God* was an important book with a message that was still relevant. My father once said to me that he considered the book his best work; certainly it is characteristic of his energy and vision. So we offer this edition partly in a spirit of grateful tribute and partly as a reminder that so much of what David Paton strove for all his life, his vision of "an authentic church, rooted in the faith and rooted also in its own time and place," remains incomplete.

In all the discussions, one point was emphasized: the book is a "classic," but one that is also very much of its own time. There would be no point trying to update the text; that would simply reduce the impact of the original. Consequently, the text has been left largely intact. The same is not true of the footnotes; these mostly discussed background reading, studies of Chinese history, Communism, recent missionary thinking, and so forth. Accordingly the footnotes have been removed, but the books discussed have been noted in the Further Reading section. Where the footnotes seemed directly relevant, they have been incorporated into the text (delineated by parentheses).

I was greatly helped in this project by a providential meeting in Selly Oak Colleges Library with Eleanor Jackson. She has been supportive throughout and was instrumental in securing a publisher. Bob Whyte was a source of wise and practical advice; I depended very much on his knowledge of the Chinese church and context and am most grateful for his introduction. Bishop K. H. Ting was most generous with his time and support; his foreword means a very great deal to all concerned with the church in China.

I discussed drafts of my account of my father's life with a number of his friends and family; their responses were most helpful, although I do not claim altogether to have followed their advice. In particular I should like to thank Bob Jeffery, Ronald Preston, Michael Paton, and my mother, Alison Paton. Others gave much advice and support in different ways: Hugh Montefiore, Lesslie Newbigin, Len Tyler, Charles Long, Franklin Woo, Martin Conway, Charles West, Don MacInnis, Werner Ustorf, and Creighton Lacy. The staffs of Selly Oak Colleges Library and Archive, Partnership House Library, the Library of the London School of Oriental and African Studies, and the Lambeth Palace Library were alike polite and helpful in dealing with what must have seemed some fairly baffling requests. Thanks are due to the SCM Press for releasing copyright and to Wm. B. Eerdmans and Klaus-Dieter Stoll for their help.

No thanks can ever repay my wife and young children for their forbearance and support while this project took over more and more of my leisure time.

David M. M. Paton,
St. Albans
December 1994

From the Preface to the First Edition

These chapters form the substance, somewhat revised, of the Godfrey Day Memorial Missionary Lectures given in Dublin in February 1952. I am very grateful alike for the welcome I received in Trinity College and for the invitation to give the lectures, which forced me to try to sort out what I have learned about the Christian mission in ten years as a professional missionary. It is a large assumption that one man's meditations on his years in China will be of use to others; and it can only be entertained because the Chinese experience cannot be called abnormal save with circumspection, and because what God has said to him has sometimes seemed to other people to be God's word to them also.

This book therefore is not for experts — who will find little that is new — but for the ordinary responsible Christian who is exercised about his Christian calling in the world. I have had in mind especially three sorts of people: my professional missionary colleagues; those faithful supporters of Christian missions overseas who are sometimes classified as old pussies or pious mice, but who are often brave as lions and wise as serpents as well as harmless as doves; and those Christians who may know little of China or of "missions," but whose care for the work of the church in their own place has enabled them, I have often found, to understand with surprising speed and penetration the different opportunities and temptations of Christians under other skies. This is one more sign of the oneness of the Christian mission; and I wish that all who love the mission could learn more and care more for the diversity of missions to which the Spirit calls a variety of people.

I write as a Catholic Christian of the Anglican obedience, who knows that his is a reformed church and rejoices with F. D. Maurice in her freedom from an authoritative dogmatic system and her implicit fidelity (which is, alas, not always as explicit as it should be) to the signs of the kingdom. Much of what I have to say will, if true, be true also for the order and works of other traditions: the necessary adjustments and adaptations can very easily be made; and I have therefore not bothered to explain or to add equivalents for "diocese," "bishop," and the like. The oneness of the mission is also demonstrated not only in our coming together in the World Council of Churches and the International Missionary Council, but also in our facing the same opportunities and dangers and being distressed by the same perplexities.

David M. Paton
Yardley Wood
Birmingham
August 1952

The Life and Work of
David Macdonald Paton

This fact of the essential and radical decay of the foundations of our society is not recognised with sufficient clarity by a large enough number of people in any branch of human activity; and this fact has confusing effects on our thought and practice alike.

(Blind Guides, 1939)

In the years since the Chinese revolution I have been trying — as parish priest, as publisher, as missionary and ecumenical bureaucrat, and then again as parish priest, to discern what might be the shape of an authentic church, rooted in the faith and rooted also in its own time and place, and how from the confusions and despairs and innovations of our age we might best move towards it.

(From an unpublished talk on Roland Allen, c. 1978)

These two characteristic utterances of David Paton, taken from the beginning and end of his active ministry, encapsulate the tensions

1

as well as the essential unity of his unusual life. Almost from the moment of his effective conversion in his second year at Oxford and from a meeting later on with Bishop R. O. Hall of Hong Kong, he felt a particular call to serve the church in China. Paton's devotion to China and its people remained a central theme of his life and thought; the renewed open contact with Chinese Christians brought great joy and fulfillment to him in the difficult years of his retirement. (Indeed, his final book, a biography of R. O. Hall, can be read as a celebration of all that the Chinese church and one of its most charismatic leaders had meant to him.) His time in China altogether radicalized and defined his view of the church and the priesthood; it confirmed and reinforced his sense of his own purpose and mission.

Active expression of that mission was, however, denied him for most of his life because of the departure of almost all foreign nationals under the Communist government. When he was at the height of his powers, convinced that his work of supporting and developing the Chinese church was truly according to God's wish, his life in China and his direct contact with the Chinese were completely terminated. This exile from a mission given him by God was the defining crisis of his life; while in a personal sense the return to Britain left his own life's work irremediably fractured. He was a man driven by and dedicated to his sense of mission, and the "missionary debacle" appeared to him as a divine judgment. The need to make theological sense of this experience dominated *Christian Missions and the Judgment of God* and led him into a prolonged reexamination of the nature of ministry and the nature of the church, a process in which he was greatly influenced by the writings of Roland Allen and F. D. Maurice.

There was, in addition, no very obvious employment that would make full use of his experience and perceptions. Some commentators have sought to take the Church of England to task for a failure to properly employ David Paton; but there is a sense in which he could never have been, despite his loyalty to and affection for the Church of England and its practices, fully engaged by it as an organization. His mission had a wider purview; he was of a world church, not a national one. There is revealed in the achievements of Paton's various jobs, and the way he defined them to embrace and enlarge his distinctive concerns, a remarkable tenacity and fidelity to his original vision: building an "authentic church rooted in the faith and in its time and place." His work in China, his active ministry in Birmingham and Gloucester, his reflections and exploration of the nature of ministry and the church, his work for the World Council of Churches and for the ecumenical movement have a unity. In his last years, when so much was denied him by his physical infirmities, he reflected much on the pattern of his life and tried to pass on to his many visitors some echo, some understanding of those experiences that had given his life meaning. In these years also came the many evidences of a marvelously renewed and vital church life in China, which confirmed for him the rightness and truth of his vision, although his health precluded his returning. Looking back over his life, he felt that his best work was embodied in *Christian Missions and the Judgment of God*. It is a book written with an urgency, a need to convey an important if uncomfortable truth, grounded in his years in China. It is his clearest and most deeply felt publication. The world has greatly changed since the years of the Korean War when the book was written, but time has not dimmed the honesty and force of his argument. The book is still important.

I

David Macdonald Paton was born in 1913, the eldest son of Rev. William Paton, a missionary figure of international importance and a founding father of the World Council of Churches, and his no less remarkable wife, Grace Mackenzie Macdonald. Paton was always happy to record his debt to his father; through his father and his many friends he received a training and an entry into the world church and an abiding conviction that "the ecumenical movement is a renewing experience without which certain things about life in the church are inaccessible." He was aware, however, in his father's career as indeed in his own, of "the unreasonably heavy and in the last resort theologically objectionable demands on the families of its servants" (unpublished talk on Anglicanism and Ecumenism).

Grace Paton, his mother, combined an intense internal and spiritual life with a shrewd, practical, and unstinting commitment to improving life for the ordinary people around her. Indeed for her, work and prayer were one. The force of her personality comes across vividly in this declaration from *The Child and the Nation* (her only book, written during the First World War and dedicated to David Paton):

The deepest need of all is not only for knowledge, but for the spiritual sympathy which kindles into a divine discontent in the face of misery and helplessness. We are too content with things as they are, even when we know the facts. If our hearts were instinct with the sympathy of Christ, even the little knowledge of social facts that we possess would render our placid acceptance of present conditions impossible.

Even as he received from his parents a pattern of religious life, so he inherited a radicalism, a disposition to challenge accepted truths and practices, that made him on occasion a difficult colleague. He perhaps idealized his parents and the family life they created; he certainly found it very painful and difficult to be separated from them during William Paton's years in India. He was very proud of his family. His brother Christopher was in the Colonial Service in Ghana and then ran International Students House; Bill, Professor Sir William Paton, was a very distinguished scientist, becoming Professor of Pharmacology at Oxford; Michael was ordained and for many years a vicar and hospital chaplain in Sheffield. His sisters, too, were remarkable: Elisabeth, to whom he remained very close, was a woman of great intelligence and religious sensibility and married Hugh Montefiore, Bishop of Birmingham; his younger sister, Catherine, a person of deep charity and humility, operated a bookshop in St. Albans and nursed her mother for many years.

Paton followed a conventional path to preparatory school and Repton. While his parents were in India for several years, he spent his holidays with his formidable Scottish grandmother in St. Albans. In later years he spoke of her without much affection, although she did pass on some understanding and even pride in the austere religious traditions and melancholy history of the northern high-lands. A warmer, more generous environment was provided by Joe and Mary Oldham, friends of his parents and important figures in the developing ecumenical movement.

Paton's headmaster at Repton was Geoffrey Fisher, later Archbishop of Canterbury. Fisher also ordained him deacon, on the eve of his departure for China, took a close interest in his career, and, while he worked at Church House, oversaw many changes and developments within the Anglican Communion, which he worked very hard to bring about. Yet throughout this long period of acquaintance there does not seem to have been real trust. Paton's thoughts on Archbishop Fisher are vividly expressed in an unpublished memoir; fundamentally, he found Fisher detached and cold, and felt that he was not the "sort of person whom Fisher would have chosen for major responsibility, at school or later." Even at Fisher's memorial sevice, the ambivalence remained: "reluctantly, but driven by a kind of pietas, I went up from Gloucester to the memorial service in the Abbey, and sat through the service — which was of a kind that was both eminently fitting and to me very distasteful — alone and unhappy, revolving many memories and trying fitfully to order them, in the presence of God."

Paton's years at Oxford were unremarkable academically, but during this time he did find his vocation. He recounted the process, in a talk he gave to the William Temple Association:

> Some time in the first half of the year 1933 as a second year undergraduate at Oxford, I went to see Bryan Green, subsequently a much-travelled evangelist and Rector of Birmingham, and at that time on the staff of the Oxford Pastorate which ministered in a definitely evangelical but non-fundamentalist way to students. I went to see him because he had been doing Bible Studies in my college and he seemed to have something. I recall nothing of our conversation, except that I came away feeling "I have known this all my life: but it has never meant anything before." Subsequent reflection suggests that the second half of that statement was an exaggeration — there was more to the religion of my childhood and adolescence than I allowed at the

age of 20. That conversation, however, was the central point of a process that had begun with the Bible Studies and was sealed by participation in a student evangelistic campaign at Coventry — when I got my baptism of fire in the woman who opened the door a crack, listened a moment, and said "We're not interested, but Johnny's in the choir." I also preached my first sermon; it lasted 35 minutes.

If I was converted, that was when it happened. The point of this rigmarole is that, being once converted, I assumed at once that I should be ordained. To be a serious Christian for someone like me and with my background led automatically to the priesthood. A year later it led me, equally automatically, to sign the declaration: "It is my purpose, if God permit, to give my life to missionary work in the Church overseas."

During the same year, he met the charismatic Bishop of Hong Kong, Ronald Owen Hall, and determined that he should work in China.

II

Before going overseas, Paton spent three years at Birmingham University as secretary of the Student Christian Movement. His devotion to the SCM and the friends he made during those three years remained with him for the rest of his life (and perhaps led him later to make the false step of becoming editor of the SCM Press). He enjoyed his role in the university and responded to what he termed "Brummie pushfulness." (He also revealed a talent for controversy; the Student Guild newspaper ran an article soon after his arrival attacking him under the headline "Who is this Mr. Paton?" This was not the last time that question would be asked!) He wrote his first major publication, *Blind Guides,* expressing his insights and response to his experience. Viewed in the light of his later work, what stands out from *Blind Guides* is the conviction, expressed in the heading quotation, that the Western liberal tradition was in crisis, in essence failing to meet the challenge either from Marxism or from the right. In consequence, new forms of thought and practice were needed. A redefinition of values and approach was particularly incumbent on Christians at the university if society were to be recalled to its Christian roots:

> In an age of scepticism and concealed despair, the primary task is that of witness to the truth, and the demand that the truth be taken seriously. If this is one of the functions of the university, then it is possible to make the paradoxical suggestion that the Church in the university, the organized representative of the Christian Church, that is, for instance, the Student Christian Movement, is called to be the university inside a university that is not a university. If a passionate concern with truth in some other sense than that of professionally valuable research (parallel to the acquisition in lectures and laboratories of professionally valuable information) is a mark of the true university, then the modern universities are not true universities at all. If the SCM, or the Church, is doing this work on as good an intellectual level as it can, then it may properly be called the university.

What was required of Christians at the university was "a more truthful type of personal relationship" and study, "to subject in such measure as is possible, everything they meet to the criteria of the Christian faith — that is, that they should think theologically about life."

The view of the Christian's role at university and the context of cultural and philosophical crisis were crucial influences in Paton's work in China and in his critique of mission policy. He was ordained deacon by Geoffrey Fisher, his old headmaster, then Bishop of Chester, in somewhat unusual circumstances — he had not undergone the usual period of theological training — to allow his departure for China in September 1939.

III

David Paton's posting in China was to Beijing (Peking), where he learned Chinese under the auspices of the YMCA. He had the good fortune to lodge with a traditional mandarin family and to observe their culture and religion. In a letter home he described a ceremony to mark the New Year:

> On the wall facing me were three portraits: father, grandfather, and great-grandfather. Beneath them was a table, with on it a small wooden casket containing the tablets of the ancestors, and in front of it a piece of red paper with the father's name in beautifully written characters. At each side was a red .candle. At the front of the table was a bowl or two of offerings of food. In turn, first the males and then the females, kowtowed three times each before the table. . . . The whole ceremony was rather impressive. I don't know precisely what religious belief the various members of the family now have about the spirits of ancestors. But at the least, even for the most secularised, it represented a profound respect for the continuous achievements of the Chinese tradition, expressed in and disciplined by its main social organisation, the family.

Such glimpses of the strength and antiquity of Chinese culture helped convince him that a real understanding of Chinese thought was a prerequisite of effective evangelism. He also observed in his letters how often even the most modest knowledge of and sympathy for the Chinese were lacking among the large foreign community in Beijing. A glimpse of a very different Chinese culture was afforded by an incident he later recalled in a broadcast radio talk:

> [Beijing was in] Japanese occupied China: that is, the Japanese army controlled the cities and the railway and the main roads, but in the hills were Chinese guerrillas. Britain was not yet at war with Japan, but most of us were pro-Chinese. Beijing is on a flat plain, but not many miles away are the western hills, and in them were the guerrilla forces of the Communist 8th Route Army, the nucleus of what is now the People's Liberation Army of the People's Republic of China. Nearby was a Christian university, Yanjing (Yenching), some of whose staff had contacts with the guerrillas. One day a message came down to us from an Englishman in Yanjing saying that the guerrillas had money

to pay for surgical instruments if someone could quietly buy up what was available in the Peking shops.

A fellow missionary did so, and David Paton bicycled out to Yanjing with the instruments, which in due course were passed on to the guerrillas. He recalled the incident to make the point that support for a principle or a cause entails practical action, that such actions may be difficult to reconcile with traditional notions of Christian behavior, but that decisions of this kind are inescapable. As a Christian, one must engage with the world.

David Paton returned to Hong Kong early in 1941, staying en route for some time in Shanghai. He was ordained priest in St. John's Cathedral, Hong Kong, by Bishop R. O. Hall. The sermon was preached by Karl Reichelt, using this text from St. John's Gospel: "As the Father has sent me into the world, even so have I also sent them into the world."

During Paton's time in Chongqing (Chungking) from August 1941 to July 1944, it is possible to trace in his letters home, in papers he wrote for private circulation, and in the article he published in the *International Review of Missions* about his work, the development of many of the ideas that informed *Christian Missions and the Judgment of God*. In the first place, he was living much closer to the life of the Chinese students among whom he was working. There were very few Europeans in Shapingba, the village and student center a few miles out of Chongqing where he lived. He described conditions thus:

> [Shapingba] is a reasonably typical example of a wartime university centre, except that it is larger than most. Chongqing University, which was there before the war, and Nankai School, which moved from Tianjin (Tientsin) just before the war, have brick buildings. Everything else is housed in mud and wattle, full of rats and bed bugs and draughts. Students sleep in double decker wooden beds, eat standing up, and supplement the vagaries of the electricity supply with vegetable oil lamps. . . . [I live] with three colleagues in a "student centre" — the second and third floors of a ramshackle and infested old building whose ground floor is divided between a bus station, a teahouse, and a post

office. It is leaky, noisy, and dirty. In it our team, two Chinese
Y.M.C.A. Secretaries, one Chinese Y.W.C.A. Secretary, and my-
self . . . carry on our work.

The poor living standards of the students, with concomitant
levels of illness, and the dislocations of war inevitably produced in
them a loss of morale and intellectual confidence. Consequently,
"liberal values" and the sense that the university has a crucial
leadership role in society — ideas that underpinned *Blind Guides*
— were at a very low ebb. Part of the problem was the Chinese
perception of the Europeans (especially the British, whose treatment of China in the hundred years since the Opium Wars was
especially resented). He analyzed these developments in a paper he
wrote in 1944 ("Liberals in the Chinese Universities"):

There is the basic resentment and sense of outrage at the "national
humiliations" suffered by a power that had been for thousands of
years supreme in its area, and which neither by temperament nor
training was prepared to face the onslaught of a power not only
technologically more competent, but acknowledging values of a
different order . . . the experience has been so shocking, and the
disasters that ensued so numbing, that the incidence of an understanding of the strength of Western power — or of the power of a
particular Western nation and the nature of Western culture — is
very small. The term "foreign devil" here has more than an abuse
value. A "devil" is by definition not wholly intelligible — a being
of power whose power cannot be precisely understood.

It is not surprising that he wondered how effective a West-
ern-led missionary effort could be in such a context. He found
himself being pushed into a leadership role, particularly in the field
of worship and doctrine, that was not appropriate, however apparently needful in the short term. He concluded that "the proper
place for foreign devils is not leadership, but working along with
and under the direction of able Chinese," such as Jiang Wen Han,
a particularly valued colleague whom Paton was able to meet again
years later in "a bear hug in which the years disappeared." He
noted that the assumption of Western leadership in church affairs

was "not confined to Shapingba but is universal, in almost all the Christian organisation" (circular letter, 1943).

A more profound problem of misunderstanding between Western and Chinese approaches, which he examined in his *International Review of Missions* article, concerned the meaning of baptism. He observed that many students regarded baptism as "a sign not of conversion to God in Christ, but of adherence to the principles of Christian idealism, with a greater or smaller infusion of religious overtones." Their view of the church was radically flawed. They "think that the Church ought to be a group of socially conscious, highly educated 'progressive' idealists: and that if they join it, it is their mission to make it so. There is little realization of the meaning of the Church as a community of sinners in process of redemption united not by education or social view, but by a common allegiance, based on a common debt to Jesus Christ."

IV

When Paton returned to Great Britain on furlough in 1944, his missionary training was in every sense complete. There were other events that marked a distinction between his first and second period of service in China. Foremost among these was his marriage, in 1946, to Alison Stewart. The daughter of a distinguished Church of Scotland missionary to North China and Manchuria, she had spent many years in China, spoke Chinese fluently, and had herself determined to be a missionary there. He had met and courted her during a short period he spent on the staff at Westcott House Theological College in Cambridge, a place where he made abiding friendships with a number of remarkable and forceful young ordinands. It was an ideal match, and their union brightly reflected their shared ideals but very different temperaments. They had three sons, all born during their years in Fuzhou (Foochow).

Another break with the past had been the unexpected death of his father, William Paton, which occurred in his last year at Chongqing. The loss remained, in a crucial sense, unrepaired; he would never be able to share and explore with his father his own missionary life, to measure his own convictions against his father's more considered judgment. He could only, as he wrote to his mother shortly afterwards, "try and repay — not crudely in terms of success — but by living as you both lived."

David and Alison Paton arrived in Fuzhou (Foochow), the largest city in Fujian (Fukien) province, at the end of January 1947. David Paton was based at the Fujian Union Theological College, helping train Chinese ordinands and Christian leaders. The Patons' letters home chronicle family news and accounts of David's work. They also reveal the manifold difficulties they and their mission work faced.

The country was in the throes of civil war; and although there was little fighting in Fujian, there were problems of hyperinflation, shortages, and general instability. The church organization itself was under some strain. It lacked the income to maintain all its schools and medical institutions; yet were it to close any of them, communities would be greatly deprived and the church shorn of its visible presence. Contributions and expertise from abroad seemed more necessary than ever in view of the dire economic situation of China, and yet it was precisely such aid and expertise that prevented the emergence of a style and scale of church life that could be sustained by the Chinese alone and that unhelpfully identified the church with foreign influence. Such considerations found mature expression in Paton's book; the "raw material" can be found in letters and diaries. Two excerpts from a diary he kept of a visit with his Bishop, Michael Chiang, to East Fujian in early 1948 may suffice:

Ningteh. A day of seeing things. The Bishop took hospital prayers and I prayers at school. Then we went round the two buildings. Both are more alive and less motheaten than Lojuan: but they are overcrowded and a little jealous of each other, and the school in particular is structurally dangerous. [He then made suggestions to improve matters.] Such a plan would have to wait upon securing a large sum of money from abroad: but an immediate necessity is a deal between the school and hospital by which the hospital lets the school have the materials it now has for a few urgent repairs to render the school building no longer actually dangerous. I should regard this last as a serious test of the reality of the Church's fellowship.

I was met by the Deacon and leper catechist, and went with them to see the leper village. Nineteen lepers in the dark and dingy asylum, and other houses with their relatives. We had a tiny little service in the little church, which depresses me (no cross, candle ends in the candlesticks, tattered hymn sheets, tattered grubby Bibles and so on and on). The lepers seemed cheerful enough, but the catechist and deacon were casual, careless and (I thought) uncaring.

However, on this trip as throughout his time in China, there were moments of profound sympathy and response to the Chinese, for example his visit to the fishing community of Fu Chu:

We disembarked to firecrackers and a crowd. The church is the only building in the place. The fisherfolk are all Christians: they live in their boats and the church and vicarage is their social centre. The church is clean and plain. . . . The faithful are poorer and more generous than most. . . . The confirmation was at 3.45-5.00 [eleven men and eight women were baptized] in the presence of a congregation of 75 men, women, children and babies: and the service was surprisingly quiet and reverent.

The organizational problems the church faced were compounded by the political challenge of a Communist government — Fuzhou was liberated in 1949. This put the church under growing pressure to prove its loyalty and patriotism by cutting links with foreign missions. It was the awareness that their continued presence in China made the Chinese church's position more difficult, and not direct expulsion by the Communist government, however, that led to the Patons' decision to leave. David Paton had long been concerned about the quality of the church's response to Communism. In 1948 he wrote to the editor of the *Chinese Recorder* (the journal of the National Christian Council) asking:

What are we going to do about Communism? I do not mean theoretically — the Christian answer is by now clear enough, I think. But how are we going to develop the essentially new forms of evangelistic method which will be called for if all the traditional forms are illegal? If we let it be, we may be faced with a new Islam — and the Christian record in that connexion is a poor one.

One result of the difficulties developing in the Chinese church over the issues of accommodating with the new regime and the position and future of the foreign missions was greater prominence for the activities of such groups as the "Little Flock," which he described in a letter home in 1949:

The "Little Flock," a purely Chinese, slightly anti-foreign, split group which preaches immersion, the imminent second coming, and the like, and is reputed to be intent on destroying the Churches of the three Missions. . . . The great attraction of the Little Flock is that it is simple, not encumbered with schools, hospitals, diocesan machinery and the like; that it is purely Chinese; and that it represents a crude simplification of the Christian life which the Fukienese like. . . . It is highly emotional in its preaching — and the Fukien Christians, starved of emotion in worship, for instance — think this wonderful; and it has a special line in relation to well-to-do evildoers, that all will be well if they hand over plenty of money.

These observations — and he went on in his letter to contrast the problems facing church and missionary structures — strengthened his conviction that the Chinese church, which he loved and to which he would remain a faithful and loving witness, could only survive if there was a radical break with the structures and ideas of the missionary era. This critique, which of course implied the withdrawal of missionary personnel and resources, was the origin of *Christian Missions and the Judgment of God*. Seeing during 1949 that the time would shortly arrive when his presence, as a foreigner, would be an embarrassment to Chinese Christians already facing hostility and persecution, he made arrangements for himself and his family to leave early in January 1951. After a difficult journey and a short period in Hong Kong while David surveyed his future and Alison had initial treatment for cancer, the Patons returned by sea to England.

V

Relatives recall vividly meeting the Paton family on their return to Britain, after what had been a fairly dreadful voyage: David was exhausted; Alison, still recovering from cancer treatment; the children, fractious and bewildered. (The eldest preferred the Chinese of his amah to English as a means of communication, which did not help matters.) The baby was immediately taken off to Edinburgh by Alison's parents, John and Gladys Stewart; while the rest of the family tried to rebuild a life in Britain, based initially in St. Albans, where Paton had been brought up. Here he was much absorbed in a round of lectures, conferences, and writing about his China experience, a process that culminated in the publication in 1953 of *Christian Missions and the Judgment of God*.

Aware that he had as yet held no parochial charge, Paton accepted, early in 1952, the living of Christ Church, Yardley Wood, a suburb of Birmingham. Alison would look back on this brief phase of her life with great affection: the children were happier and more settled; she herself was able to make a full recovery; and David was able to exercise his pastoral gifts in a setting that also allowed him some time to reflect and order his response to the Chinese experience. Some contact with Chinese Christians was still possible at this time; and K. H. Ting was able to visit England, including Yardley Wood, in 1956.

The position of editor of SCM Press, which Paton occupied for three years from 1956 and which in prospect seemed so appealing, turned out to be a false step for him. In essence, Paton, too individual and perhaps partisan in his approach, was simply not suited to the world of publishing.

A happier outlet for his abilities was Church House, where he worked for ten years. First, he was Secretary of the Council for Ecumenical Co-operation. In this post he worked very hard to promote local ecumenism and was instrumental in developing "ecumenical officers," first in dioceses and then in other churches. Through his Anglican Ecumenical Correspondence, he tried to develop a generation of young clergy committed to ecumenism. He became a major contributor to the work of the British Council of Churches and was behind the Nottingham Faith and Order Conference of 1963.

When, following reorganization, the Council for Ecumenical Co-operation was merged with the Overseas Council to create the Missionary and Ecumenical Council of the Church Assembly, he was the ideal person to bring the two together. For Paton, mission and unity were complementary, and in this new post he worked hard to bring Missionary Societies to see the centrality of unity and to establish a new relationship with the emerging new provinces of the Anglican communion. He worked hard to promote and encourage union schemes in various parts of the Anglican communion. Thus his talents as a practical, even in a sense political, organizer — and though driven hard by a vision of what ought to be, he was always aware of what objectives were possible and achievable — combined with the prophetic and visionary side of his nature to make a formidable operator.

His writings while at Church House show how deftly organizational considerations were related to the principles that ought to inform them. Roland Allen's work, for example, originally interesting insofar as it contributed a critique of missions and a view of what the church in the developing world ought to resemble, was used to illuminate current problems in the church in Britain and to suggest responses:

> In England and in Africa and in many other places, Roland Allen's ideas are being considered and applied to the problems that Roland Allen had at the front of his mind — Christians who are deprived of the sacraments (that is, of the fulness of life in Christ) because the congregations to which they belong are small, scattered or poor. Now regarded as a pastoral burden, such groups might in a different perspective become the nuclei of advance. But they are unlikely for the most part ever to be able to "afford" a full-time trained, professional minister of their own and must therefore make do with the occasional ministrations of a visitor "from the centre." That is one obvious, even glaring, example of a pastoral breakdown. There is another, in the estrangement from the Church of whole tracts of urban society.
>
> (From Paton's introduction to *New Forms of Ministry*)

He goes on to describe a possible future "missionary congregation" (i.e., lacking a professional minister and with their ministry necessarily "in common") where the common ministry "will be shared by a less churchy kind of Christian lay man and woman and a new kind of non-professional minister, working together in partnership, and prepared for their task by a training which has given much attention to the theological issues involved in Christian witness to a secular culture."

Convinced that Roland Allen's ideas had significant value and relevance to the church in a de-Christianized world, he set about with characteristic energy to popularize Allen's work, editing two selections, *The Ministry of the Spirit* and *The Compulsion of the Spirit,* and a study, *Reform of the Ministry.*

For Paton, the significance of the summary ejection of Christian missionaries from China was not in the evidence it provided of the atheistic nature of Communist rule, but in the lessons it taught us of our own failings as missionaries and Christians. And this message, sufficiently uncomfortable when applied to the mission field, he saw as having an obvious parallel in the way the churches addressed, or rather hid from, the problems of our own secularized societies. His observations on these matters were expressed with a trenchancy that was more challenging than reassuring. A fair example is this passage from *One Church Renewed for Mission,* which follows an account of his time in China:

> We live in a secular world, where Christian belief no longer has real privileges. . . . The first question about the Faith is not about Catholic or Protestant theology, or whether the Bible is inspired and if so in what way, or whatever. It is more fundamental, more personal to the individual and also to the Christian community as a body. It is: can we say with the early Christians that Jesus Christ is Lord, and can we say it out of our own deepest conviction in a way that makes some sort of sense to our contemporaries? . . . This question can only be asked and answered truthfully if we are open to the world and to the real life of our neighbours. Otherwise we simply retreat into our religious ghetto, and (now we're like Pilate) wash our hands of the world.

It was, of course, disappointing that church structures, particularly in relation to Anglican/Methodist Union, did not change as fast as he hoped. Nevertheless, he looked back on his time at Church House with some pride and, not the least benefit, a real sympathy and love for Archbishop Ramsey. (Curiously, they had both been at Repton under Archbishop Fisher, who was at this time being less than helpful to his successor at Canterbury. It made a kind of bond between them.) Later nothing gave David Paton more pleasure than the occasion when he persuaded Archbishop Ramsey to come to Gloucester to inaugurate the Via Sacra and preach in the Cathedral.

After ten years, Paton came to feel that new leadership was required and that he should resign while he still had time and energy for a new challenge. This brave decision resulted in a most uneasy period in 1969 when, no suitable approach being made, he had no living or employment to go to. In consequence, he accepted appointment as Rector of St. Mary de Crypt with St. John the Baptist, Gloucester, in the spirit of one exiled from the center of affairs. Although his appointment as Honorary Canon of Canterbury and later as a Chaplain to the Queen were a recognition of his work and the unusual standing he had in the World Council of Churches and the wider church, it is difficult not to regret the failure to find a senior role for him. (Characteristically, he ruled himself out of discussions about the Bishopric of Hong Kong when it became vacant on the grounds that a Chinese really ought to be appointed.)

However, the parish in Gloucester turned out to be a most creative and happy situation for both David and Alison. He was Rector until his retirement in 1981, and they lived in a small house in central Gloucester (Alison's "wee hoosie") until David Paton's ill health required him to move permanently into a nursing home in 1991.

As in many city center parishes, the population had moved to the suburbs, leaving the ancient and beautiful buildings in the charge of a very small congregation. A practical redefinition of ministry, a concern of his throughout his career, was forced upon him by circumstances. He faced the challenge with characteristic energy and invention. He opened out his ministry beyond his congregation to the city center, making connections between the church and people and institutions working there. He helped found the Gloucester Civic Trust to preserve and enhance the city center environment (the Via Sacra, a pedestrian route linking the several medieval churches and monastic buildings, was an early project). He was concerned, in his pastoral relations, to release the energy and gifts of the laity to the good of the church, and the moving tributes expressed at the Service of Thanksgiving show how well he succeeded. The fabric of St. Mary's was restored, uncovering a late medieval mural in the process; and an agreement was made with the Methodists to share use of St. John's, a piece of practical ecumenism that gave him great pleasure. It was very much a joint endeavor: Alison shared in this city ministry, becoming a much loved playgroup leader, member of the local Community Relations Council, and Justice of the Peace.

Paton's role in Gloucester allowed time for thought and writing on the Chinese church. For some years he, together with the former China missionaries, had been seeking to persuade the British missionary agencies to establish a full-time program on China. They were finally successful in 1972 when the China Study Project was established with Rev. Victor Hayward as project officer and Paton as chairman, a post he held until 1980. Although it was originally under the auspices of the Conference of British Missionary Societies, Paton ensured that the British Council of Churches was in association with the project and also persuaded the Catholic Institute for International Relations to become a sponsor, thus preparing for future developments and ensuring that the issue of relations with the church in China was addressed by the whole church. It was characteristic that he should be thinking about future relations with China just when China was most isolated from the rest of the world during the turmoil of the Cultural Revolution. When relationships were renewed after 1979, the ground had been well prepared. His special moment came in 1981 at a conference in Montreal when he and Alison were able to renew, after 30 years, old friendships with Bishop Ting and Professor Jiang Wen Han. Paton also continued to be involved with the World Council of Churches; he edited *Breaking Barriers*, the report of its 5th Assembly at Nairobi in 1975.

It is sad that David Paton's ill health (crumbling of the vertebrae, for which he had several operations, and latterly Parkinson's disease) precluded a return to China, which would have been a marvelous conclusion to his long years of witness. It did not prevent him from taking a leading role with Bob and Maggi Whyte, who were the China Study Project at this time, in setting up the Friends of the Church in China in 1984. He realized the importance of providing a forum for individuals and local congregations to express their concern and support for China.

Paton's life and mission had a unity and a sense of completion; and a picture of him in retirement at Gloucester, devotedly nursed by Alison, sustained by visits from and contact with British and Chinese friends, still struggling to express in conversation and writing his understanding of God's purpose, is not a bad image on which to leave this account of his life. A truer glimpse is afforded by recalling the marvelous warmth and vitality of the man. The importance of his mission, which drove him hard, never obscured his awareness of the joys and pain of this world. He loved particularly the pleasures of fellowship and hospitality. They too are part of God's pattern, as the closing words of his unpublished talk entitled "Paltry Pleasures?" vividly express:

> If the joys of married love and the intimacies of the communion of our dearest friends are so precious, how inconceivably splendid it will be to be related in that intimacy to the whole of mankind. Contempt of this world leads to a purely negative, pallid vision of heaven, and to talk about "true Christian joy" which seems not in fact to be happy at all. Rather, welcome with an ungrasping but eager gratitude the pleasures showered on you here and now because they are foretastes of what is to be hereafter and so that they strengthen you in hope of that day.

David M. M. Paton
St. Albans
December 1994

An Introduction to Christian Missions and the Judgment of God

David Paton's book stands as a major contribution to missiology in our time. It also remains as a prophetic statement about the church and China. Written over forty years ago, its insights are still important, although in many ways the world of the 1990s is very different from that of the 1950s. Although some of its observations are now dated — certainly they are sometimes expressed in a language that can seem quaint to us — the overall impact of this short and passionate work is still relevant, and it continues to challenge and disturb.

In this introduction I want to point to some of the crucial issues raised by Paton and to endeavor to show why they remain essential for our understanding of China, of Chinese Christianity, and of the church ecumenical.

Where Paton excelled was in his profound grasp of the dynamics of Chinese history and in his instinctive feel for the way Chinese people themselves think and feel. In these pages a love of all things Chinese shines through the more general argument concerning the missionary enterprise. An almost ruthless honesty compels him to speak of the failures of the Western missionary endeavor,

21

a failure in which he shared and which brought him such personal pain. Here we find a deep integrity and a radical faith. For friends and colleagues the remarkable qualities of the man were always apparent. How else can we explain the enduring respect felt for Paton in China? Certainly he was not always easy to work with, and on first acquaintance many were fooled by his bluff exterior and his apparent membership in the Anglican establishment elite. For him Anglicanism was a vital part of his makeup, but for carefully thought-out theological reasons.

I should like to discuss the book in the light of Paton's relationship to three topics: the Anglican tradition, Chinese culture, and the missionary movement. I shall then go on to look at Christianity in China forty years later in the light of Paton's insights.

Paton and the Anglican Tradition

I write as a Catholic Christian of the Anglican obedience, who knows that his is a reformed church. . . . (p. xiv)

If we must keep the faith ever before us, we must keep the world ever before us, too; for it is God's world. (p. 42)

Paton was heir to a theological tradition that can be traced back to Richard Hooker and his "Laws of Ecclesiastical Polity." Bishop Lancelot Andrewes and the Caroline Divines of the seventeenth century perhaps gave finest expression to a theology that was both reformed and catholic. The world and its social and political structures were not to be despised, but rather to be the arena where the Christian works out his or her faith, calling the world to sanctification. Paton's own theology was profoundly influenced by this generosity of spirit that delights in all that is good in human culture and society. The natural corollary of this emphasis is that theology should arise from an encounter with the surrounding cultural context. In this Paton was far ahead of his time, anticipating the theological agenda of today. Anglicanism also informed his thinking on matters of polity, but he avoided the Erastian temptation that has sometimes infected Anglican thought, where in effect the church becomes subordinate to the state. At the same time his background meant that Paton understood far better than missionaries from non-established churches the need to enter into dialogue with the state. He knew the ambiguities of Christian living in the world and suggested that the relationship of church to state should be one of "critical dependence" (p. 57).

Paton was impatient with those who would seek to be independent of relationships with the state, calling this "futile self-deception." He understood the dilemma that faced Chinese Christian leaders in 1949 and the difficulty of establishing even a relative independence in the context of a totalitarian state. He knew from his own experience of Chinese Communists that they would demand uncritical dependence, and he understood the immense pressure that was put on Christians to conform.

It was this realism that enabled Paton to avoid the danger of a Pelagian view of culture:

> But let our confidence be sober, and rooted in a faith that knows all about evil. (p. 45)

He was well aware of the dark side of human nature and society. He wrote of the "joint achievements of sin and stupidity" in the world, and he was equally conscious of the impact of the same sin and stupidity on the church, which as a human institution is also fallible and in need of judgment. Perhaps the influence of his parents was responsible for the introduction of a vital element of Reformed theology into his Anglicanism!

We have seen in the first section of this introduction how Paton was heir to a powerful ecumenical family tradition. His own ecumenical theology was rooted in the work of F. D. Maurice, that outsider in Victorian theology. Maurice always looked for the "signs of the kingdom" in the midst of the complexities of social and political life. He declared:

> There is a Catholic side of the Gospel as well as a Protestant; a side that has reference to Society as well as one that concerns each of us. We . . . are bound to recognise both. . . . We shall not do justice to one truth if we let go of the other. We shall

not make that stronger by weakening this. We want each in its fullest strength. (Lincoln's Inn Sermons II, 15)

This sums up beautifully Paton's own standpoint, a standpoint that enabled him to look at the experience of Christianity in China free of a number of the ecclesiastical and cultural presuppositions of many missionaries, mission agencies, and home churches.

Like all truly great men, Paton was rooted in a living tradition, which in his case was Anglican; but he never allowed his commitment to one tradition to fail in generosity toward other traditions and insights. As the reader will soon discover, this did not prevent him from making some fierce judgments where he deemed that Christians were in danger of turning the gospel into a new legalism and the church into a sect. We will look again at what he has to say on this, for it is still relevant to understanding Christianity in today's China.

Paton and Chinese Culture

There is in fact no such thing as a pure gospel: it is always incarnating itself in a culture. . . . (p. 56)

Paton saw with remarkable clarity of insight just where the Western mission to China had fallen short. At root it was a failure in theology. Little of the theological reflection undertaken by either missionaries or Chinese Christians showed much awareness of the cultural context. The only really promising Chinese theologian in the years leading to 1949 was T. C. Chao, but he was to fall silent before the Revolution and to end his days unsure of his belief in God. In other circumstances Chao's thought might have come to maturity and have helped in the reconstruction of Chinese theology. Yet perhaps his thought is not lost, for there are indications that he continues to influence a new generation of theological teachers.

Paton's sense that Christianity had missed the point when it came to developing a theology that related to China was shared by his friend and mentor Bishop Ronald Hall of Hong Kong. Hall had written in 1942 a small pamphlet, "The Missionary Artist

Looks at His Job." He suggested there that to understand China you needed to know about her art and poetry rather than about her religion. Paton thoroughly agreed. This sense of a culture and the development of a profound respect for that culture is the hallmark of a successful missionary as far as Paton was concerned. When the opportunity came to set up the China Study Project in 1972, Paton helped to ensure that its focus was on the whole Chinese experience. The reopening of links between the British and Irish churches and Christians in China after 1979 and the way this relationship has been shaped owe a great deal to Paton's broad and truly ecumenical vision.

Paton acerbically sums up Chinese Christianity as he knew it in the twilight years after the War:

> There are Chinese intellectuals: most of them have no theology worth speaking of. . . . There are orthodox Christians: they are mostly simple-minded fundamentalists, or educated clergy whose thought remains woodenly in western categories. There is a vacuum. (p. 81)

He knew from his own experience how Chinese Christians had remained aliens within their own culture.

There were, of course, those who claimed to be indigenous. There is an important sense in which groups such as the Little Flock and True Jesus Church can legitimately make this claim. Not only were they self-supporting with indigenous leadership, but they also shared in the ethos of Chinese village religion, a characteristic that helps to explain their continuing importance today. However, on another level they were influenced by the conservative theologies of fundamentalist movements in the West such as the Brethren.

Christians of the mainstream denominations were also strongly influenced by conservative theologies brought by missionaries, both Protestant and Catholic. The twentieth century saw the influx of liberal Christian ideas, often associated with the American "social gospel" movement. This influenced quite a few Chinese Christian intellectuals, and many came to sit lightly both to church structures and to any strong doctrinal position. This was sometimes called the "Christian Movement." The rising nationalist tide and a deep concern with the problems of the poor amongst educated Christians meant that, not surprisingly, many in the "Movement" retreated from engaging with hard theological issues into a watered down "social gospel."

Paton's work in both Chongqing and Fuzhou made him conscious of the gap between the majority of Christian converts and educated Chinese. Although large numbers of intellectuals were educated in mission schools, they sided with the Communist Party rather than the church. The long-term effect, as far as Christian intellectuals was concerned, was the abandonment of the field to Marxism. Paton could, nevertheless, sympathize with the Movement, which provided a haven for those who wished to escape from "missionary sterility." He also appreciated that a number of young intellectuals joined and came to lead the indigenous sects in reaction against the missionaries and "the sterility of the church and the badness of the times" (p. 69).

Paton's sense of a major theological failure was confirmed by the tragic fate of Chinese Christian intellectuals in the Peoples' Republic. By the early 1950s the best representatives of this Movement were coming to see the superficiality of the humanist versions of the "social gospel" and were seeking a more deeply rooted theology. But it was too late — the immense political pressures that first manifested themselves even as Paton wrote his book prevented serious theological reflection. These pressures were to reach an unprecedented level in the ten years of Cultural Revolution after 1966, although in the end it was this experience that led to renewed opportunities for Christianity in China.

Marxism was in fashion in the 1940s and 1950s. It is important that we take cognizance of this fact when reading Paton's words on the need to encounter the Marxist challenge. It is too easy in these days after the Cold War to dismiss Marxism as an outmoded ideology. Paton appreciated why:

in China . . . [the Communists] unquestionably have the support of the majority. (p. 49)

He understood the force of nationalism and the ultimate absurdity of those missionaries who thought that they could remain unpolitical when the missionary is "by his very existence a political fact" (p. 54).

Paton was intensely aware of the fate of the poor. He saw that it was the Communists who were tackling basic problems of public health, malnutrition, and education. So he writes:

> Our rural service work prospered therefore in a merely superficial sense, for it never made fruitful contact with the moving forces in Chinese society. (p. 71)

Communism was not to be simply ignored or dismissed. What is needed is:

> a knowledge of Marxism and of Marxist ways of thinking and feeling. . . . A purely theoretical acquaintance with the academic case against Communism is worse than useless. (p. 54)

Anticipating some of the insights of liberation theology, Paton felt compelled to accept the seriousness of the Chinese Communist critique of the Western presence in China. His judgment that "we failed to take seriously the fact that Chinese society was ripe for revolution" (p. 71) was all too correct.

Paton was nevertheless no Marxist. In his view Marxism was fundamentally flawed. He recognized that the appeal of Marxism to the Chinese was not really on the level of philosophy. But it filled a vacuum, and therefore an authentic Chinese theology would need to encounter Marxism before it could mature. The reason was in part a matter of sheer common sense — China at this point in her history would follow the Communist path. Neither Christianity in its Western forms nor liberal social democracy had been able to put down deep roots into Chinese culture and society. That is why he spoke of the need both to encounter Marxism and to master it.

Paton and the Missionary Movement

The world of the missionary in China during and after the Second World War was disturbing and uncertain. The disruption of church

life by the Japanese in large areas of China was considerable. David
and Alison Paton's lives were typical in this respect. So was the sense
of vocation — a sense that stayed with him to the end of his life.
Where he was atypical was in his reaction to the experiences of war
and revolution and in his capacity to stand back from his immediate
situation and to seek to discern the will of God. Here the strong
influence of Roland Allen can be discerned. He found in Allen a
kindred spirit in which a faith both biblical and catholic dared to offer
radical solutions where others were hidebound by an inability to
rethink even the inessentials of past practice and tradition.

After the end of the war, the escalating conflict between the
Nationalist "Kuomintang" led by Chiang Kai-shek and the Communist guerrilla armies of Mao Zedong meant that former patterns
of church life could only be partially reestablished. The missionary
community was divided between conservative Christians who reacted
to the upheavals of war and revolution by seeking to deny their reality,
seeking to create an alternative religious world, and liberal Christians
who continued to pin their hopes on Chiang Kai-shek and to assert
the possibility of reform. A few, including some who had found
themselves living in Red areas and a group working with the
YMCA/YWCA, expressed support for the Chinese Communist Party
and its nationalist intentions. Most, however, were not prepared to
face the reality of the Communist upsurge; and when the possibility
of a Communist victory became apparent, their reaction was one of
disbelief and gloom. The triumph of Mao and the Communists in
October 1949 was therefore greeted with almost universal condem-
nation by missionaries and their home boards and churches.

David Paton's criticism of the missionary movement was much
misunderstood. Perhaps in the context of the treatment meted out
to individual missionaries in the 1950s it was hard for many to
listen to a radical critique of the movement in which they had
shared, often at great personal cost. The reaction can be easily
understood. In 1952 few could go along with Paton's words that:

> Our mandate had been withdrawn . . . the time for missions as
> we had known them had passed; that the end of the missionary
> era was the will of God. (p. 82)

In fact, the 1950s and 1960s seemed to confirm the views of those who had roundly condemned Paton for his supposed betrayal both of his fellow missionaries and of Chinese Christians. The reports of denunciation meetings, of the imprisonment of Christians critical of the new government, and of the steady decline in church attendance made it difficult to accept Paton's verdict. *Christian Mission and the Judgment of God* was published during the Korean War in the heightened atmosphere of the Cold War. It was small wonder that Paton's pleas that Marxism needed to be taken seriously fell on deaf ears.

Reading the book today, we can more readily accept Paton's radical critique while acknowledging at the same time the great contribution of many individual missionaries to the Chinese people. One result of the more open situation in the 1980s and 1990s has been that many former missionaries have been able to return to visit areas where they worked. They have been welcomed with deep love and affection by Christian communities that have long been independent of foreign influence and control. Bishop K. H. Ting, president of the China Christian Council, was able to speak publicly during 1994 of the contribution of the missionaries to the development of Chinese Christianity.

It remains true, however, that some of the key issues identified by Paton in 1953 have not been adequately addressed by the Protestant church in China today. We must look at these in a moment, but before doing so we need to acknowledge something else identified by Paton that is of fundamental importance. Toward the end of his chapter "The Christian Mission Today," his words are truly prophetic for the experience the Chinese Christians were to undergo in the years of suffering:

> Anyone who has been subjected at all deeply to the life of the Communist Empire must find among other things that his Christian faith takes on a new meaning and depth; that many old and dull truths suddenly become fresh, exciting, matters of life and death; and that he is forced to stand and deliver what is in him as he has never been forced before. In this crisis, a man discovers what he really believes, often with results that disconcert both

him and his friends. Some move rapidly far closer to God; others apostatise. (p. 59)

Chinese Christianity Today

How then are we to apply these insights to the interpretation of the contemporary situation of Christianity in China? I would like to discuss three areas: the nature of Chinese Christianity, current theological trends, and ecclesiology in China today.

The Nature of Chinese Christianity

The thirty years between the founding of the Peoples' Republic and the reemergence of church life into the open in 1979 were years in which Chinese Christianity appeared to go into terminal decline and then emerged to confound both Chinese and foreign observers by the rapid growth in numbers in the 1970s — a trend that has continued to this day.

There can be no doubt that one important effect of the stripping away of all formal structures has been a strengthening of the Christian base in home and village. Paton was clear that it was in the village and the home that Christianity would put down strong roots:

> Experience in China suggests that it will be increasingly prudent . . . to put the main emphasis on Christian training in the congregation and in the home where it properly belongs. (p. 96)

The remarkable growth of home worship gatherings, now numbering in tens of thousands, is the most telling testimony to the correctness of this insight. One can also see how it was the dedicated work of missionaries throughout rural China that sowed the seeds of this growth. However, the successful creation of a church that can be described as "enculturated" has brought to the fore some of the innate problems that Paton saw so clearly.

Heirs to the pietism and fundamentalism of a large section of the missionary movement, the majority of Chinese Christians, whether Catholic or Protestant, see faith as a private matter between the soul and God. This leaves little space for the prophetic dimension. Preaching is narrow in its focus and sometimes over-emotional in content. Moreover, as far as Protestants are concerned, there is rarely any sense of the church as a nonlocal entity; and contacts beyond the local congregation are usually limited to practical matters. Worship, even in large city congregations, lacks a liturgical framework; and there is almost no theology of the sacraments.

Paton was not content to see Christianity in such a way. While concerned to see the development of a popular Christianity, he warned of the dangers of sectarianism:

> Rejecting the foreign church of the missionary and uninterested in his church history, [the sects] reject in effect the corporate fellowship in time and space of the Christians, and do not heed the lessons which the fellowship has learned. (p. 94)

The Catholic Church in China, while sharing the conservative ethos of Protestant Christianity, does retain a strong sense of the church as catholic and this in spite of the serious divisions caused by the enforced break with Rome in 1957. But in different ways both major traditions have not addressed the underlying theological issues that are now urgently in need of being tackled. Here too Paton's analysis can be helpful.

Theological Trends

Throughout the long years since 1949, Chinese theology as a self-conscious discipline has hardly progressed. Chinese Catholics have moved from a preoccupation with the past to a new interest in post–Vatican II Catholicism, but so far little original theological work is being done. On the Protestant side, a number of theological educators associated with the Nanjing Seminary are involved in a limited program of theological reconstruction; but they remain isolated from the predominantly conservative churches and home meetings throughout rural China.

Bishop K. H. Ting, President of the China Christian Council, and others in Nanjing have written and spoken of the need to introduce the concept of the Cosmic Christ into Chinese theology as a corrective to the emphasis on individual salvation. Here may lie the seed for future development, but for the moment there is scant evidence of theological advance among Christians in general. As we have already noted, pietism and biblical literalism are the norm. Alongside this there is a considerable emphasis on healing miracles. This has to be seen as a response to the present lack of medical support in poorer communities. The danger of seeing religion as the means to prosperity is also apparent in some places. Paton was well aware of the danger:

> Chinese fundamentalism is in its basic drives altogether too prone to feel about "salvation" as if it were the same sort of thing as the prosperity here and hereafter which is the goal of ordinary Chinese village religion. (p. 95)

Society in China is still dominated by the Communist Party, but the values now purveyed are no longer Marxist, nor even socialist. Was Paton correct to suggest that Marxism needed to be encountered before it could be mastered? Have not the capitalist values of the marketplace now taken over? Certainly the tide of history has moved on, and no one can seriously claim that Chinese Marxism as an ideology is now making a creative contribution to the development of China. Paton, of course, never suggested that Marxist philosophy had much impact on the Chinese people. It was the Communist Party as the purveyor of nationalism that provided the impetus to the revolution of the 1940s and 1950s. The power of this organization is still formidable, but it no longer commands the moral authority it once had.

The church in the 1950s soon discovered that, as Paton had warned, Christians could have no role in the Marxist experiment:

> The assumption of independent initiative by sectional interests cannot but be undesirable to the Communist authorities. (p. 86)

On the whole this remains true today with the crucial exception of the economy, where the Party has ceded much of its control to private enterprise. It is a situation that is ripe for eventual political upheaval. In this unstable and uncertain environment, many are searching for new values. Christianity has the potential of making an important contribution to the society that will emerge from the ruins of Communism. The vitality of local Christian life is an inspiration to the worldwide church, but the question remains as to how far it has been able to come to terms with the new situation. Moreover, despite its successful enculturation, it has hardly begun to come to grips with what it means to reflect theologically on contemporary Chinese realities. What does it mean, for example, to relate in a creative but critical way to the surrounding society? Relationships to government are still too often defined as accommodation or tacit resistance.

Another aspect of the problem is the uncertainty of most contemporary Chinese as to what constitutes Chinese identity beyond a purely racial definition. The terrible destruction of traditional culture over the past forty or so years has led to a profound ignorance of the past. The return to the village has been a necessity. The capacity for real development here must not be underestimated. In spite of his criticism of the sects, Paton endorses the view of Roland Allen that in the early church the "source of heresies was not the inrush of more or less illiterate converts (the prospect of which so disturbs us), but the speculations of learned men" (p. 80). Unfortunately the greatest threat to the true development of Chinese rural Christianity comes from outside attempts to impose theological straightjackets and to foster denominational differences.

A further issue relates to the gap between rural and urban life in China, which is clearly reflected in the church. Suspicion of urban church leaders among rural Christians remains a real problem. Students who go from villages to train in urban seminaries frequently meet with suspicion when they return to exercise their ministry in their home churches. Women pastors are less likely to be welcomed in the countryside. This separation into two distinct worlds is likely to pose a continuing difficulty for the normalization of church life.

It is in the cities that we find a fascinating and crucial development that, while superficially reminiscent of the "Christian

Movement," is very different in its theological seriousness and in its evaluation of Marxism. I refer to the remarkable emergence of a growing number of intellectuals who are showing a deep interest in Christianity. For them Christianity offers some answers to the problems thrown up by the collapse of Marxism. Few show any interest in the churches, which they find pietistic and unimaginative. No doubt there is here an element of traditional intellectual snobbery, but for our purposes what is of considerable interest is that here we find a group of people who have encountered Marxism and are now moving beyond it. They find consumerist values shallow and are looking for ways to reconstruct society on the basis of humane values, which they associate with the Christian understanding of the person. They see the Christian view of personhood as placing equal value on both individual and community, and find this of immense importance in a society that has always tended to put society before the individual with dire consequences for human rights.

Bishop K. H. Ting has suggested that the future of Chinese theology perhaps resides with these intellectuals. One day it is to be hoped that these nonchurch Christians and the masses of ordinary believers will find in each other the means to create a mature Chinese theology.

Church Order

Perhaps the most disturbing aspect of contemporary Chinese Protestant Christianity is its failure to take the doctrine of the church seriously. A good deal of Paton's work is concerned with this question. His discussion of the growth of sectarian forms of Christianity in China remains very relevant to the situation today. One of the ongoing results of the missionary movement is the tragedy "that catholic order and the freedom of the Spirit" (p. 79) are opposed to each other. It was, in Paton's view, a theological failure by the whole Western church that led to the export of sectarianism to China.

The post-denominational church so often spoken of is the product of political necessity rather than of ecclesiology. It is true that today the majority of Christians in China probably have no experience of denominations, but the lack of a sense of history combined with years of isolation has led to a situation in which a de facto congregational order has emerged and where nonlocal church structures are seen as merely expedient from an organizational point of view. The Trial Order for Church Use adopted at the Fifth National Christian Conference in 1992 is little more than a statement of organizational goals — and even these seem unable to be implemented effectively. In such a situation fragmentation and disorder are all too common, frequently seeming to mirror similar disorders in the secular sphere.

Chinese Catholics remain divided by questions of authority. Protestants are finding it increasingly difficult to hold very different traditions together in one framework. There is a distinct possibility that we will see the reemergence of denominations — something that the de facto existence of groups such as the Little Flock, the True Jesus Church, and the Seventh Day Adventists suggests is already underway.

The inability to solve the problem of church order is producing serious internal conflicts within the Chinese church that are only compounded by the resolute efforts of the state to control religious activities. The bad effects of this have become more and more obvious in the 1990s. Reports of conflicts within local churches; the arbitrary exercise of authority by church leaders acting with virtual autonomy from national or even provincial structures; the imbalance between rich and poor churches; the uneven implementation of government religious policy; problems in persuading local churches to accept younger pastors — these are but some of the difficulties arising from the present confusion.

Paton believed strongly that Protestantism was destined to fragment wherever it failed to address questions of ecclesiology. For him Anglicanism at its best represented a tradition that valued both catholic order and Protestant spontaneity. He writes:

> The catholic episcopate, the catholic priesthood, the catholic sacraments are essential, and our distresses abroad and at home are in part due to our failure to value and use them properly. (p. 103)

However, alongside this we need to place remarks such as this:

> A sacramental system that is exalted but practically unusable falls
> into contempt. (p. 79)

He was, after all, a tireless ecumenist and had no time for
denominational niceties. Nevertheless, it is to be doubted whether
many in China would understand his concern; and this suggests a
tragic dichotomy in the story of Christianity in China. The great
gulf that exists between the Catholic and Protestant churches is a
significant pointer to the failure to hold catholic order and the
freedom of the Spirit in a creative tension. The lack of dialogue
between the two traditions means that both are impoverished:

> It would not have happened if we had not exported to China
> our own torn and mutilated Western post-medieval Christian
> tradition. (p. 79)

Conclusion

It would be wrong to conclude on this somewhat pessimistic note.
Despite all the problems, Christianity in China today is full of
vitality. The growth since 1949 has been remarkable. At a very
conservative estimate, the total number of Catholics and Protestants
has grown from around four million in 1949 to around twenty
million in 1994. Whatever political and social upheavals may lie
ahead, Christianity has shown that it can survive even amidst the
most extreme adversity. We must not underestimate the power of
grassroots Christianity. New leaders are emerging even if few are
known outside of their own localities. The stripping away of denominational structures and the growth of lay leadership make a
return to an overclericalized and hierarchical church unlikely, even
in the end for Chinese Catholics. Roland Allen's dream, shared by
David Paton, has been partially realized in China. Whether there
can ever be a role for foreign missionary personnel is another
question. The discussion has moved on since 1953.

It is remarkable how many of Paton's reflections remain of

immediate relevance today. The issues he perceived as important in 1953 are still central to the future of Christianity in China.

It is no wonder that Paton himself was able to pursue his vision through to the end of his life. He met Bishop Ting for the last time in the nursing home in Harpenden in the summer of 1991. Few words could be exchanged, but few were needed between two men who knew and understood each other. In this very personal moment, one sensed the confirmation of what Paton had striven for so passionately and a sealing of his life's work. He died one year later.

I should like to conclude on a very personal note. As David Paton's health deteriorated through the 1980s, I was privileged to spend long hours with him discussing the contents and themes of my own book, *Unfinished Encounter.* It was a humbling and exciting experience. For those who did not have such an opportunity, the reading of *Christian Missions and the Judgment of God* is not a bad substitute. Beyond all else, to savor this gem of a book is to learn afresh the real challenge of the gospel.

Bob Whyte
All Saints Tide
1994

*Christian Missions and
the Judgment of God*

I. The Christian Mission Today

The Christian mission is what the New Testament calls a "mystery." It is what St. Paul calls *the* mystery — a secret hidden within God even before the creation of the world, but now made known to men and women of faith, whereby all nations are to be gathered up and presented to God through Jesus Christ (Col. 1:26-29). This gathering up takes place in the Church, the mystical body of Christ. The mystery has been unfolded according to a divine plan; prepared by the vocation of the Jewish people; and substantially realized by the mission of the Incarnate Word Jesus Christ, who by his ascension introduced human nature for all eternity into the sphere of the life of the divine Trinity: and this plan is to be accomplished among the various peoples of the world during the time between Pentecost and the Second Coming. The Christian mission is thus anchored in dogma; it is a result of what ordinary Christians *believe*. It is God's plan, God's activity; but because God became man and took up manhood into himself, it is God's will embodied in active obedience on the part of the Christian individual, the Christian group within the church, and the Christian church as a whole — we are all involved in it, all of us, in our various callings.

We shall be concerned here mainly with the Christian mission as it is expressed in what used to be called "foreign missions"; and with a wide range of practical matters more than with dogmatic theology. It is the more essential, therefore, to fix our attention at the outset upon the faith, seeing the faith not so much as a set of propositions held in some precise form by ourselves and in that form to be defended against all comers, but as the record of what God does for the salvation of the world.

"The salvation of the world." Archbishop William Temple once remarked that our Lord might be less interested in "religion" than is the curate of the parish church. The proper concern of the clergy is with religion in the narrow sense: they stand to the laity for God. The proper concern of the laity is with their work in the world: they stand to the world for God. Both the professionally religious and the laity need each other. If we must keep the faith ever before us, we must keep the world ever before us, too; for it is God's world.

It is God's world, and it is one. To it God's church has one mission. Although there are diversities of gifts and varieties of calling — the broad distinction of clergy and laity can be almost indefinitely subdivided, as we well know — there is only one body, to which with these diverse callings and gifts all belong. One moves with no sense of an intellectual or spiritual customs barrier from wondering about the future of the Christian mission in China to talking with those who wonder about the present tasks of the Christian mission in Paris or Sheffield. This is one world geographically. We have grown familiar with this idea, and with the fact of the worldwide church. "The nations" to whom the gospel is to be preached are many; and even in that purely geographical sense, there are some yet unreached. But the nations have their own life and culture, and these also must be penetrated with the gospel, and led by it to bring their glory into the kingdom. England is a Christian nation in a sense that India, for example, is not; but those who care most for God are most aware of the ranges of English life that are not yet baptized, much less growing in grace. The extension of the mission is not only geographical, but it is also sociological.

It is in fact here, in the revolution created by the spread throughout the world of western technological method, that there lie the most pointed challenges for Christians. There used to be a rough-and-ready, but true, distinction between the unchanging East and primitive Africa, and the changing, industrial, socializing West. That sharp distinction is now blurred. Education, health services, science, industry, the social service state — in one form or another these things are the agents of revolution anywhere. Even Tibet has been liberated by a Communist army; even Greenland housed Allied troops during the war; the tiny sheikdom of Kuwait is involved in the immensities of oil capitalism. The tempo varies: the place on the road to some sort of totalitarianism or some quite new sort of free society reached by this land or that differs widely. The forces are the same. We live in one world; and we have to it one mission.

The illustrations given are symbolic: they remind us of problems rather than achievements, of evident dangers more than of cheering opportunities. It is easy today to lose heart. Indeed, far too many people have lost heart. They would not admit that they have no hope in this world, but the implication of their comments on current affairs, their attitudes toward events is precisely that. We know that "now abide faith, hope, and love," but in our own experience there is not much hope. We hope to get by without World War III or a runaway inflation; we hope that if these things do occur, we shall somehow survive with those we love. We do not actively hope for God to act among us: we are rather resigned to the heavenly will; and just as the lawyers use the term "act of God" to mean some calamity too great for man to foresee or to cope with, so "God's will" is likely to be something unpleasant. Our hope, where we have it, is generally for heaven hereafter, when the worst that this world can do is done, and we emerge purified by our long-seeming winter into the sunshine of God's eternal presence.

If this is how in fact we tend to feel — however loyal to the full Christian faith we may be in our formal statements — it is worth asking ourselves frankly why we feel like this, facing the question whether this world of ours, though doubtless formally God's world, is not temporarily, at least, in the power of the Devil and his angels?

I do not think I am fanciful in discerning among some of those who most earnestly plead against the Christian social movement a feeling that there is something fundamentally intractable, inscrutable, mysterious about the world, and that no more can be hoped for than an heroic protest in the name of Christ, made in obedience, but with no sort of hope that anything can come of it. I hope I am not wrong in saying that there is nothing Christian in such an attitude. It savours of the Paganism that saw behind the world a kind of ironical malice; that made Polycrates throw his ring into the sea and called the Furies the Kindly Ones, if haply they might so be appeased. But we stand outside this world of darkness, for we have learnt that all things were created by the eternal Word, who is Christ Jesus. We know, in the Pauline phrase, that it is in Him that the whole universal order of things consists or holds together. Those who have come to know that, know in consequence that they are in their Father's house. It is a big house and they have begun to explore only a little of it. It has great reaches and some of them are still shadowy. But it is His house, all of it.

(William Paton, *The White Man's Burden*)

"It is His house, all of it." It is also in a prize mess. It is worth remembering, however, that not everyone is as gloomy about the state of the world as those who, like most parsons, having received an education in the humanities combine an interest in public affairs with an almost complete lack of training in the disciplines which provide the techniques for understanding and dealing with our common problems: economics, industrial management, diplomacy, nuclear physics, and soil chemistry, for example. It is said of nuclear physicists that the more they know about the future possibilities and present developments of work in atomic physics, the more frightened they are; but it does not seem to be true of scientists generally — whether their professional concern is with pure research or with technological development — that they are as depressed as Christian publicists often are; and the same is true of the immense army of workers in administration, the social sciences, and education and psychology — not to speak of members of the Communist party — who all tend to regard the present as in one sense or another the doubtless very painful birth-pangs of a new order. Moreover — mental attitudes apart — careful, detailed studies in modern factories do not, for example, support the thesis that modern mass-production industry offers only a soul-destroying monotony, destructive of man's creative instincts. Such work would doubtless have that effect on those, many of them Christian intellectuals, who hold these views: it need not, and often does not, on those actually at work in such industries.

There are thus reasons for discounting some of the gloom we inevitably feel upon reading the headlines, especially if we approach matters in a factual, scientific manner, with the head rather than with the nerves. Educated Christians are especially prone to nervous strain because we are mainly middle class, and we suffer from nostalgia for a past which we understood, in which we were at home, and in which the gospel and the church were both more respected. Whether the "good old days" were in fact "good" is not part of our present enquiry: in any case they have gone forever. Nostalgia for a more orderly and friendly past is bad, even if the past were in fact better than the present, because nostalgia tends to blind us to what the present ought to become. Wiser is the attitude we get from the best and most responsible politicians; a sober realistic confidence is preferable in general to fatuous optimism or fatuous pessimism.

It is preferable because it is more congruous with the Christian faith, and is in accordance with the common sense one expects in God's world. Here as elsewhere, faith and reason are not opposed. Just as the world has always been God's world, from its origin in his creative wisdom — but *we* have not seen it so until the advance of science and technique have made it possible for us to move about it freely — so from the same operations of the cool, instructed human reason, we may derive tested reflections that will sustain us in our struggle.

But let our confidence be sober, and rooted in a faith that knows all about evil. Our world is one world — in God's design, and in human technology. It is also divided by Curtains of Iron and Bamboo. The joint achievements of sin and stupidity are today remarkable — so remarkable that we may wonder whether there is not a further mystery of iniquity. The writer's father, whose rejection of the pagan idea that the world is governed by evil or chance or fate has just been quoted, also said once that passing through Shanghai in 1935 had finally convinced him of the existence of the Devil; for in the appalling nexus of evil in Shanghai, there seemed to be something at work beyond what could be accounted for by the follies and wickedness of mankind.

The Devil, then, must also be given his due. Mr. C. S. Lewis suggested in the preface to the *Screwtape Letters* that it is equally dangerous to our race to display either too much or too little interest in the Devil. Interested too deeply, we assign to the operations of the Devil events which can be adequately explained by common or garden sin, abnormal psychology and the like, and indulge in these orgies of witch-hunting that stain the history of the church. Scornfully enlightened, and ignoring the well-authenticated phenomena of demon-possession (whether in the Gospel accounts of Palestine or in modern Africa or China), we allow the Devil a wider field for his operations by the very fact that we are off our guard. Both these attitudes are common; and not to be imitated. We may usefully recall that the original Greek of the petition "deliver us from evil" may also be translated "deliver us from the Evil One," and preserve that proper agnosticism without which there can be no true faith; only, if we allow for the operations of the Devil, let us be very clear that God is sovereign.

The consideration of the Devil is not an irrelevance. There are too many today who feel him to be on top, and the influence of astrology and the other modern superstitions affects us all more than we may suppose. But at the highest estimate, he is not the center of the picture; nor is he our first consideration when we consider the mystery of iniquity.

The center of the biblical teaching, most especially in the prophets, about evil in history is that what appears to us to be unmitigated evil may in fact result from the wrath of God. "The wrath of God" is today a dangerous phrase, for it is often thought necessarily to imply a sort of personal vindictiveness. That is a misconception. Fire, for example, warms you or burns you according to how you handle it. Jesus was life to the Eleven; and disaster to Judas. Did not he himself say, "I came to cast fire on the earth"? God comes to us in Christ, as he came to the Twelve; in each of us there is something of the experience of Peter who denied the Lord, of Judas who betrayed him, of John who loved him, and of all of them together who so often "understood not the saying, for it was hid from them." Where we obey him, he is known to us in mercy; where we rebel, in wrath. The mercy and the wrath cannot be separated: in wrath he remembers mercy.

The use of the biblical term "wrath" is inescapable, though we must be aware of the risk of misunderstanding. It is not merely ecclesiastical conservatism that bids us to retain it, but the knowledge that so much impoverishment is due to the premature discarding of ancient Christian terms that we have not understood and have therefore thought to be without meaning or truth. We do better to live with them till they yield their meaning. The "wrath of God" is eminently a phrase we shall do well to live with, until with its aid we become reconciled to the mysteries of God's working today; and this applies to us educated Protestants of the Anglo-Saxon industrial West who have such difficulty in understanding the worldwide revolt against our hegemony.

The turbulent processes of history then — to put in other language our argument to this point — are the scene of the unfolding of the purposes of God. We who are charged with the proclamation of the gospel are to obey him and to witness to him, not in some small percentage only of our interests which can be salvaged from the enemy, but in the whole of life. We, his people, are one people. His world is one world. But because he is greater than we can conceive, his workings will not be fully intelligible; because we are sinners, they will be to us frequently both disconcerting and uncomfortable; and because all the universe is his, he will be found in the secular as well as the religious world, in Communist China as well as in Oxford or Tunbridge Wells. He will, in fact, appear to us in judgment; and the executors of his judgment may surprise us. He will appear to us, and the understanding of the ways of his workings will require of us faith indeed, and also such instructed reason, such sanctified common sense, as we may be able to attain.

Where then, in more detail, shall we look for the workings of God? Within the church, certainly. We shall not ignore or underestimate the fact or the importance of the faithful worship and witness of millions of ordinary Christian people, sweetening and enlightening the life of the communities in which they live. They are there today, as they were in what are sometimes called "ages of faith"; and in our anxiety over the state of the world, we should not overlook them and their influence — indeed, if we cannot honestly feel that we belong with them, our first efforts should be to learn to do so.

But the church is not only the recipient of God's merciful grace. It is also the object of his judgment, and his wrath. No clear distinction can be drawn between the light of the church and the darkness of the world. Nor can the beneficent operations of God's Holy Spirit be confined within the limits of the church.

We ought indeed to expect to find the works of God in such things as the advance of knowledge. Knowledge of the physical universe is not to be thought irrelevant to Christian faith because it does not lead to saving knowledge of God. Insofar as it is concerned with God's creation, physical science is a fitting study for God's children. Moreover, the advance of scientific knowledge does negatively correct and enlarge theological notions — at the least, the geologists and astrophysicists have helped us to rid ourselves of parochial notions of God and filled in some of the meaning of such phrases as "almighty." In addition, the result of the technical progress is to enlarge the area of human freedom. Progress in this sense does not make us better; but it does enlarge the range of choices before us, and thus requires us to act responsibly, choosing good instead of evil, God instead of ourselves, where previously we acted more or less automatically because we had no choice. The possession of leisure is one example, the invention of more or less reliable contraceptives another. Millions of people now enjoy sufficient leisure to face them with a choice about how to spend their time; whereas before, it was very much a matter of work or starve, and little time for anything else. The general availability of contraceptives combines with the reduction of infant and maternal mortality to endow the use of our sexual powers with a new freedom.

These freedoms are new, and they contain wide potentialities of good and of evil alike. So far they seem to be good, fruits of the work of God the Holy Spirit. They enable us, indeed, not to cling to what is now the old-fashioned doctrine of automatic progress, but to believe that besides the obvious progress in technological complexity, there is in history a progress in human mastery of the environment that carries with it an increase in human freedom; and they confirm the Christian conviction that "secular" life is not neutral or hostile to the purposes of God. These freedoms themselves also make clear the two-sided nature of God's dealings with us. Each increasing freedom is an opportunity for virtue; it is also an opportunity of newer and more profound and far-reaching forms of vice. Science itself is evidently a vehicle of God's judgment, the means both of his mercy and of his wrath.

If this is true of the "secular" world as a whole, it should not surprise us to find that God is addressing us in the political and social revolutions at its heart, which so disturb the life of the church. One of our main themes, indeed, is that the ending of the missionary era in China by Communist *force majeure* is to be understood as the execution of the will of God, albeit through those who not only do not recognize him, but even deny his existence. This has proved a disconcerting doctrine, and it will be well to pause a moment and examine it.

Our thesis is that God's judgment today is being executed upon his church by political movements which are anti-Christian. Of this almost worldwide movement, the Communists are the spearhead. They are not everywhere in control; and in Africa, for example, they have only recently started work. It can also be argued that in the long run nationalism and the social service state and the industrial enterprise will prove to be the permanent forces, and that the Communists are important mainly because the Marxist philosophy of dialectical materialism seems to thousands in the West and millions in the East to be the only philosophy and political theory that can fulfill the yearnings of nationalists and give to the masses the fuller life that they believe modern science and technology make possible. These considerations should make us pause before concentrating attention exclusively upon Communism, especially in its philosophical aspect; they do not affect the fact that at the moment it is the Communists of whom the West is scared, and the Communists who appear to be the instruments of the wrath and therefore — since the two can never be finally separated — of the mercy of God.

It is unpleasant to have to see things in this light, because we in the West are aware that in Asia certainly, and to a considerable extent in the West (especially in France and Italy), it is the Communists who have the initiative. They have a political program that is attractive to the population and a carefully worked out technique for attracting and consolidating support and for winning power. And, for example, in China, so far at least, they unquestionably have the support of the majority. We lack these advantages, and in compensation seem to have only a superior technical military potential (which we cannot always effectively deploy) and a belief in liberal capitalist democracy as a superior way of life, whose relevance to the quite different circumstances of countries that have never been through the struggles of the seventeenth and eighteenth centuries in the West is not always obvious. Has the West to add to its difficulties the demoralizing thought that it is our enemies who, after their own fashion and though they do not know it, are "on God's side"?

"On God's side" is a difficult phrase. "Who is on the Lord's side?" begins a well-known hymn, and it is hard to answer. It is safe indeed — more, it is required of us — to seek to serve God's purposes: it is wrong to be too self-confident. We are, in Luther's phrase about the Christian man, *simul justus ac peccator:* "righteous, and also sinners." We had best avoid classing ourselves or our enemies as "on God's side," and concentrate on seeking to understand what he is doing.

To say that the Communists are the executors of God's judgment does not in any case imply that they are "on God's side" — as the careful reader of Isaiah 10 will discover. The Assyrians are there defined as "the rod of mine anger"; but it is also laid down that they will in their turn suffer for their "proud heart" and "high looks." The identification of the Communists with the Assyrians might suit us quite well — after all, in the end they disappeared from history, while the chosen people remained. But there are other possibilities: Isaiah 45, for example, defines the Persian Cyrus "who has not known me" as the instrument — this time not of God's wrath, but of his mercy upon the Jews, for his vocation is to restore the chosen people to the promised land. There are many Christians in Communist countries who see the role of their non-Christian governments in terms of Isaiah 45 and not Isaiah 10. There are also, for example, the symbols used in the Book of Revelation for the Roman Empire — the great beast, the harlot drunk with the blood of the saints. These would doubtless suit some of us best of all.

We are not here primarily concerned with the detailed evaluation of the role of Communism (though we may observe in passing that the Communist term "liberation" is a nice example of the ambiguities of the divine working among sinful men); and it is improbable that any one of the symbols of past ages will be precisely appropriate. Our immediate point is that to think of the Communists as the executors of God's judgment should not strike us as strange if we have read our Bibles. The same study should free us from the assumption that God will always be on our side whatever we do, will always protect his church from temporal evil, or that he is only concerned with the faithful believers. It was precisely his concern for the wicked Ninevites that so distressed the prophet Jonah. In the same sort of way, it is a mistake to suppose that to pray for one's enemies is to give comfort to the Queen's enemies and so an act of treachery; or that to pray for the Cabinet logically involves your giving your vote to the Government party. The petition "O God, save the King" is logically at least compatible with the conviction that the King's salvation may require that he be replaced by his heir or by a republic — as the Christian minorities in the kingdoms of Egypt and Jordan may recently have been discovering. Once again, what we are or should be concerned with is God and his will, not with our own safety.

Therefore, facing God at work in his world, and meeting him in judgment rather particularly in the revolutions of our day, what is our attitude to be?

It is natural to us to seek to defend ourselves: to admit, of course, that we have our failings, but to insist that much of our work stands and has been blessed by God. This attitude is the prime obstacle to the gospel in your heart and mine; and its name is "pride." When the devout Christian examines his conscience with a view to confession, he does not make excuses and expound to an attentive Almighty the numerous extenuating circumstances. He seeks to repent, with as few half-measures as his spiritual stature permits. What is right for the individual should be right for society as a whole; although, for reasons with which events since 1933 have made us all familiar, a society finds repentance much harder than an individual. (It should not have needed Hitler and others to teach us what was already in Holy Scripture.)

Had there existed in Samaria in the time of the prophet Amos a Samaria Council of Churches or a Royal Institute of International

Affairs, it might, in the course of its ordinary business, have published a report on the State of Church and Nation, or Israel's Foreign Policy. Such an official report would have admitted the blemishes upon Israelitish society and the occasional failure of its foreign policy. There would be links, that is to say, with the same subjects as they are handled in the word of the Lord as it came to the prophet Amos. This is speculation, for all that has come down to us is what Amos reported of God's word. But it seems a not unreasonable sort of speculation. And the point is this: those who see in Chinese Communism the judgment of God do not claim to be latter-day Amoses: they claim that we all stand in the same sort of position as Amos's hearers. If this is so, then we need no temporizing and face-saving, or even balanced and fair-minded appreciations of our strengths and weaknesses, but thoroughgoing repentance. Moreover, there is a practical disadvantage about making excuses for oneself; it cuts the nerve of reforming action. I stay as I am. If the situation requires drastic reform as the condition of survival, it is not a good thing to remain unreformed.

That is why the accusation that the prophets had to face, of being traitors and defeatists, was beside the point. Everything hinged on whether they were right in their understanding of the facts. Jeremiah was tormented by his inability to prove that he was a true prophet and the optimists false prophets. The only proof was in the march of events. Nor is it a guarantee of truth to prophesy disaster, to counsel submission: submission in some circumstances, as Pétain found, may be as false as resistance in others. Once again, only time can show. The one final clue we have is faith — ability to "read the signs of the times." For this ability, one necessity is technical information — the prophets seem to have been better equipped in this regard than some contemporary preachers; the other is a knowledge of the counsels of God, which is born of faith.

In this attempt thus to read the signs of the times either for Christian missions or for the future of the European way of life, one conclusion is inescapable: it is that, estimable in some respects as are our present ways and considerable as have been their achievements, if we continue in them we shall meet disaster. The first thing to do is to really face this most unpleasant fact; the second is to think very, very hard what to do about it.

Prophetic repentance is the first requirement; a steady nerve is the next. A large number of people have lost their nerve in face of the Communist advance: this is true equally of those who in effect wish to concede the game to the Communists, believing them to be invincible, and of those who wish to visit upon us the horrors of a preventative war. In more religious terms, we are tempted either to believe that in face of the Communist attacks upon missions there is nothing to do but withdraw, or to retire into millenarianism and hope that the possibilities of the third world war may prove to be the beginnings of the End, and that the war itself may be taken up into Armageddon, or else to retire from the world and leave it to the Devil because the times are so evil. To face the world today, to find God's path through it, will take a very steady nerve indeed, and this steadiness may be required all our lives.

Repentance and a steady nerve are not unrelated. It is only when we are freed from personal preoccupations and the need to defend ourselves against attacks on our conscience that we can afford to look at the facts. The penitent man alone can trust in God; and since he trusts in God, can afford the open mind which will look fairly at all God's facts. On the one side of such an attitude is the defeatism we have sketched — the too ready assumption that the battle is lost; and its source is lack of faith. On the other is an optimism, which sometimes masquerades as "balanced judgment," whose source is a faith, but not so certainly a faith in God.

It is with these considerations in mind that the church must address itself — in the best of our people is already addressing itself — to the evaluation of Communism and, more especially for our missionary concern, of the Communist attack upon imperialism. This last is the central issue for missions. We have been accustomed to believe that whatever may be said of other aspects of Western activity in Africa and the East, the contributions of missions have been both objectively beneficent in their effects upon the people, and subjectively sincerely loving in their source in missionaries' motives. The Communist attack — which is in essence an attempt to discredit missionaries by attacking their *bona fides* — is thus peculiarly bewildering and distressing to the very large numbers of missionary-hearted people who have never previously supposed that they should bother their heads about politics and economics.

No adequate study of these issues is here attempted; but it may be in order to suggest some of the conditions of an answer. First is the Christian realism of sinners forgiven by God which we have already discussed. Second is a knowledge of Marxism and of Marxist ways of thinking and feeling; this is not easily acquired except by contact, preferably prolonged, with serious Marxists. A purely theoretical acquaintance with the academic case against Communism is worse than useless. Third is a clear-sighted understanding of the real nature of the missionary enterprise as it exists today — not as we like to think it exists; and with this should go a grasp — which is oddly lacking sometimes even among otherwise impeccable evangelicals — of the doctrine of justification, of the fact that God can use sinners for his glory.

There is, however, a further condition, which requires somewhat more elaboration. This is that we shall have something like an adequate understanding of the relations of church and state — in themselves, as they affect missions, and as they affect our own mission in particular. The customary attitude amongst missionaries has been a simple-minded assumption that "we have nothing to do with politics," which echoed an equally simple-minded regulation of the missionary societies that the missionary will refrain from any political activity.

This attitude has been sincere, but it has had little relation to the facts of the matter; and this contrast is a further illustration of the depth of the remark that it is easy to be sincere, but desperately difficult to be truthful. In a country that is being revolutionized by the invasion of the Western world, a Christian missionary who comes from the Western world, be he as harmless as a dove, as unpolitical as Jane Austen, is in himself by his very existence a political fact. The Japanese in their occupation of North China rightly realized that by their very presence American and British missionaries were sabotaging the "New Order in East Asia" even if they never said a word against the Japanese, for they were in themselves symbols of a world that opposed the Japanese empire; and in themselves symbols of the hope that the Japanese New Order would in the end be destroyed by that other world. In the same way, the Chinese Communists desired in all good faith to eliminate Christian missionaries who came from the anti-Communist West, for they were convinced that the missionaries were centers of resistance, even if that resistance were only passive.

But the issue goes deeper than that. Much more critical attention needs to be paid to the relations of mission and church to the government of the country and to the government of the country from which the mission comes. Our interest in these matters has usually been confined to the repercussions of government policy upon mission institutions or activity; sometimes this has been varied by a simple acceptance of one's own country's policies, and more rarely with an enthusiastic and uncritical acceptance of the policies of the government of, or of a party in, the country of one's adoption. None of these is enough, though the last of them, when it is as deep and as genuine as it was in the case of Charles Freer Andrews, the friend and supporter of Gandhi, can become a profound and fruitful way of identification, and so a presentation of the Incarnation; but if it lacks religious depth of this kind, it can readily result in the missionary's becoming the virtual mouthpiece of some party or other. The anti-type of Andrews is the retired China missionary who spends his time urging support of Chiang Kai-shek and the Kuomintang.

The elements of a more satisfactory understanding are an adequate evaluation of the political parties and trends in the country in which one works; an adequate evaluation of the policies of one's own country if these greatly affect the country of one's adoption (as they usually do if one is British or America); and some sort of doctrine of the relations of church and state. This is a large order, and it is idle — and indeed improper — to require that every missionary work the whole question out *de novo* for himself. It is reasonable to ask that the missionary societies should work out a body of doctrine and be aided in the task by the universities and divinity schools.

What all this means to the missionary in practice may be illustrated by example. I am, let us say, a missionary in Nigeria. The school in which I teach is a mission school, and my salary is paid through the mission by the government (which is controlled in the end by the Colonial Office in London). What is my effective reply to the African nationalist who says I am simply an agent of the imperialist government? Alternatively, what other means are there at present for pressing on with African education? What attitude do I adopt, and on what grounds, to the various Nigerian parties? None of these questions can be adequately answered without a theological as well as a scientific evaluation both of British colonial policy and of African nationalism, and a critical appreciation of the relation to them both, not only of the mission (which after all is temporary, for as Henry Venn put it, all missions look to their own euthanasia), but of the African church, which will be there after we have all gone and which may be gravely embarrassed — indeed, often has been — by an uncritical assumption that British views of the government will be shared by Africans.

Dr. K. S. Latourette has shown in his *History of the Expansion of Christianity* that the church has never been planted successfully in a culture previously alien unless there was also a profound and extensive communication between the Christian culture from which missionaries came and the alien culture to which they went. This indeed is what we should expect from a religion of incarnation. There is, in fact, no such thing as pure gospel: it is always incarnating itself in a culture; and one might even say that Dr. Latourette is putting in other, less shocking phrases the Communist case that missionaries are the secret agents of imperialism. It is evidence, at all events, that the Communist charge cannot be simply dismissed; and it is likely that the only effective reply to the Communist critique of imperialism will be what has been called a "theology of imperialism." Lest this phrase be considered scandalous, it should be added that this theology may turn out to be a demonology. That is, if, as we have argued earlier, Communism and the immense Communist empire is part of God's purposes, so are capitalism and imperialism — or at least have been, as Marxists will admit when not engaged in propaganda. The remaining question — and one of quite desperate importance — is whether capitalism and imperialism (in other words, the Western Christian nations) still have as nations a positive role in Africa and the East, and if so what it is.

We must hope that this question can be answered in the affirmative. An affirmative answer will require not only the labors of thinkers, but also the willingness of large numbers of young Western Christians to spend their lives in other lands, and to spend them in a very different manner from that which has been customary among empire-builders in the past. But even if there is a positive future for us, we cannot remain content with the attitudes of the recent past. We may concede that the church and the mission are inextricably involved in the community and the state; we must nevertheless hope for — and indeed work out — a more critically independent attitude than has been common.

This at least is true of the mission when conducted by foreigners. The church of the country is another matter. Except where it has been, as in the early centuries, a tiny minority, the church has usually accepted and worked with its government or has, as an infrequent alternative, embraced the revolution. And it is often difficult to see what else could be done. Should the bishops have declined Constantine's support? Remembering their background, is it reasonable to think that they should have done so? Under different forms, this is a living question today in China. Nor can the issue be evaded by specious pleas by those who deplore establishments and fight for the separation of church and state. American missionaries are not more detached from the American way of life and the total operations of American society in the world than their English Anglican colleagues from the English equivalents.

In the face of all this history, the plea of independence appears to be futile self-deception. There can be no real independence. The same history does, however, suggest the desirability of a more critical kind of dependence. Constantine's bishops probably had no option but to support Constantine in return for his support of them. A maturer body of principles of ecclesiastical polity than they in fact had any chance of framing might, however, have prevented their accepting the persecution of non-Christians. We, on our part, have a vastly greater experience upon which to draw; and of those to whom much is given, much is expected.

What can be the basis of a relative independence, or a critical dependence? Compressing into a paragraph a complicated theological issue, which is one of the principal divides between the Catholic and the Protestant points of view, we may advance the following propositions: First, that any *elaborated* Christian politics or Christian sociology will turn out to owe more to the dominant ideas and still more the dominant social structures of its time or origin than to the gospel. Second, that this does not mean that all social

and political systems are equally sinful and therefore equally irrelevant to the faith. Some systems are better than others: medieval
feudalism can reasonably be held to have been preferable to Hitler's
National Socialism. But history has so far disclosed no system under
which it is totally impossible to obey God and witness to him.
Third, that the church and the state have different functions in the
community, and the roles of bishop and of statesman do not call
for the same qualities — and both would be the better for remembering that the artist and the scientist also have their callings.
Fourth, that the gospel cannot be applied to the world like stick-
ing-plaster over a cut; and that normally, between the gospel and
a set of current political policies or possibilities, there have to be
developed middle terms, which can on the one hand be reasonably
considered to be deductions from the Christian faith, and on the
other can serve, as the gospel alone cannot, as touchstones by which
practical policies can be tested. Such a middle term is the family.
The health of the family, socially speaking, is something the Christian faith requires us to foster; and policies that tend to destroy or
weaken the family are so far anti-Christian. But it has also to be
observed that in some countries the defense of the family can
become a cover for the defense of a particular type of family
organization, and so the defense of a particular social order may
be adventitiously assisted by specious Christian argument. This is
a sign that our middle terms will need critical examination, not that
they are invalid. Fifthly, the church will always recall that as she
seeks the ever-deepening incarnation of the gospel in the world, so
this can only be complete if it leads to the transfiguration of that
world; and finally, that all her activity, as all the world's, is only "till
he come," when all things will be made new in a sense we can now
but dimly apprehend.

This point, that all our life is provisional in one sense at least,
introduces the question of the relation of the crises of our day to
the final crisis, the end of all things, and of our own Christian
activities to the final consummation of God's purpose.

"The judgment of God" is a phrase that has occurred several
times already. It is not only left-wing Christians in Communist
countries who feel themselves to be living in an apocalyptic Day of
the Lord, a time full of darkness and the crashing down of venerable

institutions, of confused battles and garments rolled in blood, and yet a time that can truly be referred to as "this great age," the dawn of a new world. Not only those whose minds and imaginations have been stirred by the prophets of the Old Testament are stimulated by the events of our time to faith and hope. Anyone who has been subjected at all deeply to the life of the Communist empire must find among other things that his Christian faith takes on a new meaning and depth; that many old and dull truths suddenly become fresh, exciting matters of life and death; and that he is forced to stand and deliver what is in him as he has never been so forced before. In this crisis a man discovers what he really believes, often with results that disconcert both him and his friends. Some move rapidly far closer to God; others apostatize.

It is surely not wrong to believe that this sort of experience is in a figure a foretaste of the Judgment: that although it is always true that "now is the judgment," we are today privileged to experience it more sharply than usual. Whether or not this supposition is legitimate, those who have passed through an experience of this kind will assuredly no longer remain content with the postponement of the Judgment to a future so distant as to be irrelevant, and will no longer suffer their Christian faith to be emasculated of the conviction that what we do as Christians is dynamically related to God's whole plan.

As we ask this question, we are faced with the debris of one dead doctrine and the competition of two extremely alive ones. The dead doctrine of progress sustained our fathers in the carrying of capitalist democratic culture to most parts of the globe. Its core was the conviction that in thus extending the range of western liberal culture and developing its assumptions, they were in effect establishing on earth that which would grow into the kingdom of God. Some put it sharply but unbiblically: "building the Kingdom"; others, of a more secular turn of mind, echoed J. A. Symonds' hymn, "These things shall be." That whole view exists today only as debris, for it has foundered on the rocks, not so much of human sin, as of the contradictions and complexities of the very western culture that was the substance of its belief.

It is otherwise with Marxism. From one point of view, Marxism is the older doctrine of progress brought up to date by absorb-

ing — indeed giving pride of place to — the contradictions of capitalist society that cause the liberal failure of nerve. The Marxist at
all events believes that in history there is a movement — dialectical,
stormy, checked here and there, but finally and certainly advancing
to the goal of the classless society, which may be postponed, but
cannot fail of achievement, and in which all human strivings and
yearnings will be fulfilled. And of this movement he is the servant.
Whatever his personal distresses and failures, he is justified, for he
is on the side of history and humanity. He understands the drift of
history and sets himself scientifically to advance it. The day may
not dawn in his time, but that it will dawn he knows, and he knows
also that its dawning is hastened by his labors.

On the other side of conventional Christianity are the adventist
sects. These also see in the events of our time a revolutionary
situation and set themselves to take advantage of it. But it is a
revolution of another sort altogether: it is the End of which the
New Testament speaks, and the wars and civil wars, the famines,
riots, and disturbances are the signs of the End, the harbingers of
Armageddon, as the explosions of atomic energy are the fulfillment
of 2 Peter 3:10. These men also have hope in history; and their
preaching takes on a renewed and practical urgency as they seek by
their witness to discover the elect and to save them from the wrath
to come.

The weaknesses, not to say falsities, of these views are obvious:
more important are their strengths. They have in common certain
convictions, which are conditions of any eschatology that is to satisfy
men. The answers are wrong, but the questions to which they are
false answers remain; and the needs which they seek, but in the
end fail to meet, are real needs.

We must believe in a movement, or a Person, active in history,
greater than ourselves, giving to history its meaning, and providing
for us a cause to live and die for. We must believe that what we
do in fidelity is dynamically related to the unfolding of that
purpose. We must not have things wholly taped. It is significant
that in all eschatologies there is an area of imprecision, of mystery.
"The workers lose every battle but the last," and there is no
guarantee — however painstaking and thorough your scientific
social analysis — that the situation you believe to be the revolu-

tionary situation for which you have worked and longed is in fact that situation. You may demonstrate that the End is nigh, you may even by juggling with figures in Daniel or Revelation, or with the measurements of the Great Pyramid, prove that the End will occur this year or next, but when it does come, your faith is not always shattered.

With these suggestions in mind, let us turn to the New Testament. It is unquestionable that the very early Christians expected the early return of the Lord, and his delay distressed the Thessalonian Christians. Second Thessalonians 2:6 suggests that some obstacle is holding up the beginning of the End. The most likely obstacle is indicated in Matthew 24:14: "And this gospel of the kingdom will be preached throughout the whole world, as a testimony to all nations; and then the end will come." This may well be related to St. Paul's desire to get to Spain, which was the end of his world; and we should also take into account his teaching in Romans 9-11. Why had the Jews apparently been rejected? His answer was that they had not been, but "through their transgression salvation has come to the Gentiles . . . a hardening has come upon part of Israel, until the full number of the Gentiles come in and so all Israel will be saved" (Rom. 11:11, 25).

The End, that is, waits until the gospel has been preached to all nations: conversely, Christian witness is dynamically related to the consummation of God's purpose in history.

This is not, of course, more than the beginnings of an answer. It takes up only some of the hints in the New Testament. There are many others of which no sensible account can now be given (the word "sensible" being designed to exclude, for example, the identification of "the son of perdition" with Marshal Stalin). In the last few decades the New Testament scholars have been concentrating on eschatology, but the theologians have not yet paid much attention to their labors; and ordinary church life tends to be either quite oblivious of the End, or else unduly wrapped up in it, like those Thessalonians who neglected their work and were rebuked by St. Paul.

Superficially it may look as if the view we have sketched makes too much of "missions." We shall not think so if we recall the universal character of the Christian mission and are faithful to the promise of God to sum up *all things* in Christ. If the "powers that be" (the realm of politics and government) are "ordained of God" and are to be subjected to Christ when he "shall be all in all," then the political activity of obedient Christians is not less related to the completion of God's plan than more conventional types of Christian witness. By the same token, we are not required to decide that the saved will be few, or many, but can leave that in God's hands, where it belongs.

The New Testament seems to combine with the conviction that what we do is a part of God's plan a taciturnity about the precise relationship of what we do with the consummation of God's purpose. "Lord," said the seventy on their return from a preaching tour, "even the devils are subject unto us"(much as returned missionaries might point, as they sometimes do, to such successes as have attended their labors as signs of the imminence of the End). But Jesus replied, "In this rejoice not, that the spirits are subject unto you, but that your names are written in heaven." We are to be concerned, that is, only with being like God and doing his will because we are his, leaving the issue entirely in his hands (see Luke 10:17-20).

But before he said that, Jesus said, "I beheld Satan falling as lightning from heaven." We do not experience now a foretaste of Judgment which, because it is compounded not only of wrath but also of mercy, is also a foretaste of victory. The mystery hid from the beginning in God has been declared in Jesus Christ; it does not yet appear what we shall be, and we see now in a glass darkly, but we do see. We experience at once his coming in the flesh and his coming in glory; and we go out to meet him, to receive whatever he may give us, to do whatever he may command.

II. Missions under Judgment

This chapter will be very critical of the missionary work of the church. It is necessary, therefore, first to recall what has been said about the necessity for repentance. When a disaster has occurred, nothing is really wise, or even kind, save ruthless examination of the causes. If you have cancer, it is not in the long run a kindness on the part of your physician to fob you off with kind words and soda bicarbonate, when early recourse to the surgeon may save your life.

Secondly, the diagnosis that you have cancer does not preclude the possession also of excellent lungs and superb feet, nor does it mean that your constitution has always been weak and sickly and good for nothing, and that there is no hope for you. Criticism of missions, then, is not a denial of much faithful work now or in the past, nor of a great measure of success. There are, after all, the younger churches. The gravamen of such charge as is made is not that the younger churches do not exist, but that they are weaker than they should be; not that our forefathers were wholly wrong and have left us in an impossible position, but that often we have continued things which were once right and are now wrong. These lines from the hymn are worth continual pondering:

New occasions teach new duties:
Time makes ancient good uncouth.

Ancient good, not ancient evil. Many ancient goods have become very sadly uncouth today; and not only in China, nor only in what used to be called the "mission field," are there new occasions and new duties.

Thirdly, what we have to say is drawn from experience in China. Those concerned with other areas are probably already somewhat wearied of being instructed in the right way by the China missionaries; and this is intelligible in itself and perhaps also an indication that some of us from China are more anxious to show that if we were failures, so is everyone else, than to walk humbly with our God. But it is also evident from the conversation of missionaries from other countries, and still more of African, Indian, and other national Christian leaders and workers, that a very great deal of what was true in China is true elsewhere. It is unlikely that missionaries in India, for example, would be wise to find out what our policies were in China and do the opposite, still less that displaced persons from China are capable of giving them detailed advice. It is our duty to declare what it seems to us God has said to *us* in our experience; the duty of others, including people at home, to listen to this and seek to hear what God is saying to *them*. It has also to be remembered that the reports from China are the reports mainly of missionaries, and that our knowledge of what the Chinese are thinking today is very limited indeed. Try as we may to see things from the Chinese Christian angle, we shall inevitably distort their picture; and this is a serious disqualification. On the other side, it is true that it is not missionaries, but Indian and African Christians, who are fundamentally responsible for their church; and it is they, rather than our missionary colleagues, who need to learn from China; for it is to them that the word is really addressed.

Let us begin with the charge that Christian missions are a part of the total imperialist aggression of the West, and especially of Britain in the past and America in the present, upon Asia and Africa.

The pages of history dealing with our activities east and south of Suez in the eighteenth and nineteenth centuries cannot be read today without shame. There were, of course, mitigating features of various kinds: missions generally made a better showing than some other aspects of Western penetration, though this point must not be sentimentalized. It is also possible to interpret the whole story in a detached impersonal way as the inevitable and mutually uncomprehending encounter of a crude and dynamically expanding culture with other static cultures lacking the equipment to enable successful resistance. There are values in this sort of interpretation, in which Professor Toynbee's *A Study of History* abounds; it encourages a compassion for the struggles and defeats of humanity, which is one necessary, but by no means the only, element in a mature Christian conception. But if we interpret the original Western invasion of Asia and Africa in terms of blind, ineluctable historical forces moving on their way like the chariot of Juggernaut, and therefore refrain from moralistic abuse of our empire-building forefathers, we have to play fair and see in Asian nationalism an equally blind counterattack on the West — the inevitable march of historical forces that we ourselves released, and deny ourselves the pleasure of condemning what may seem to us the impious dreams of domination of the Chinese Communists, the crazy irresponsibility of Persian nationalists, or the criminal folly of Egyptian politicians.

All this may reasonably enter into our thought, but we shall be wise to pay special attention to our own shortcomings. We are often forbidden in Holy Writ to judge others; nothing is said to discourage us from self-examination and confession. Of these the sin that has most deeply wounded Asians and Africans, and rendered them almost unable to see anything good in us, is what Kipling somewhere refers to as "the triple-ringed uninterest of the Creed that lumps nine-tenths of the world as heathen." It is the uninterest, borne of contempt for others and of self-satisfaction within ourselves, that has most exacerbated relations between us. The upper-class Englishman has been guiltiest of all; but in general it holds for all of us and is by no means confined to, or latterly even specially characteristic of, missionaries.

All this makes it a valuable exercise to look at the recent history of India or China, for example, as it appears to Indians or Chinese. Such accounts may not be wholly fair — they will not be: nor are our own. But it is useful and illuminating to see ourselves as we appear to others; and we have also to remember that whatever the rights and wrongs of the case *sub specie aeternitatis,* what Chinese and Indians and Africans think is an increasingly important objective fact, irrespective of whether they are right or wrong. The failure to perceive this elementary truth has landed the British in considerable difficulties at various times and places in the last few decades, and it continues to be characteristic of us.

The old charge against missions used to be — it is still made everywhere, though in China it has now been supplemented by a more radical attack — that missions were a part of the whole imperialist aggression of the West. This charge cannot be evaded in face of the inclusion in the unequal treaties of clauses, extorted from unwilling Chinese authorities, establishing the right of missionaries to travel, acquire property, and preach the gospel in the interior of China. Nor can it be denied that most missionaries held that China's only hope lay in full Westernization, and that in its political and economic aspect, this could only be carried through with Western loans and Western personnel. And a good many missionaries have, in fact — though decreasingly of recent years — had very close relations with their countries' embassies.

But these actions and attitudes and others like them are no longer the main issue. The main charges are now two:

First, that Christian missions and the churches they have fostered have throughout presupposed and disseminated the capitalist culture of the West and have been allied with such forces in China as were sympathetic to, or could be the tools of, the capitalist and imperialist West; and that therefore, objectively speaking, the mission and the church were fundamentally reactionary forces, opposed to the true interests of the people, and hangers-on if not active agents of the interests of Western powers, and would remain so even if, as missions have for decades declared to be their final aim, the mission were itself wound up and all missionaries retired, leaving the church wholly responsible.

Secondly, that whatever may have been the formal aim of missions, their actual policy was such as not to foster, but to preclude, the development of a genuinely dynamic, self-governing, self-supporting, and expanding church.

We may as well admit right away that these charges are in general sound; and that the second, which is in the long run the more important charge, was made with unanswerable force by Roland Allen in his *Missionary Methods: St. Paul's or Ours* (1912) and *The Spontaneous Expansion of the Church and the Causes which Hinder It* (1927). To Allen's case we can add little, save more recent examples of the diseases he diagnosed at a later stage of their progress; and we would urge the study of both books, and especially the first, upon all who care for expansion of the church, not only overseas, but also at home, where the problems are often even more intractable.

The entire structure and ethos of the church in China was, with minor much-paraded exceptions, Western. Prayer books are in the main direct, not to say crudely literal, translations of the original. The union hymn book in general use contains 62 original Chinese hymns out of 512, and 72 Chinese tunes. Church architecture is mainly a matter of brick boxes, with odds and ends of embellishment from the Gothic revival. One could not expect high office — succeed a missionary or become a bishop — unless he had at least a Western-style education and preferably rejoiced in a Western degree. The structure of diocesan organization and accounts was based on Western models, and is grotesquely complicated for the numbers involved and the relative simplicity of church life.

Missionaries, with few exceptions, maintained a Western style and standard of living, in which they were joined by those of their national colleagues who had attained the education and the financial means to do so. Chinese Christian leaders, with some exceptions, have been notorious for their poor grasp of Chinese literature and philosophy, and have often been more at home in the English language and in Western culture. In the more educated sections of the church, even more than in the *compradore* class as a whole, men and women have looked to Europe, and still more to America, as the source of civilization. (The *compradore* class is a phrase used to describe the intermediaries between the invading West and the structure of Chinese government and life, including Chinese church workers, government agencies, etc.) They come back fascinated with the latest toys and gadgets of Western civilization; and if they have been able to afford them, their houses are cluttered with them.

The educated Christian leaders were inevitably regarded by the Communist authorities as mainly a reactionary force; they were, however, known to be very discontented; and they possessed a high degree of acquaintance with and mastery of Western scientific and technological methods. They are therefore in need of indoctrination and reform, and because of their potential contribution, worth a good deal of attention. In those facts lie the principal causes of the pressure upon the church in China today.

It is not otherwise with the church's institutions. Our schools were started to produce subordinate professional workers for the church; they expanded to become the principal training-grounds from which were recruited those who filled positions in the world of the *compradore* — the Customs Service, the Salt *Gabelle*, the Postal Administration, and the foreign firms, the Chinese banks, and the business houses that were associated with them. Many of the more ardent spirits were stirred by their shame at their country's weakness and their anger at the wrongs it suffered at the hands of foreigners. They considered that the education they were receiving might possibly be designed for the gradual reform of Chinese society, but if so, for reform in the interests of the West, in whose *bona fides* they had lost all trust. They did not believe it could assist the revolution of China in the interests of the Chinese people. They went over, in the end, to the Communist Party, in which there are surprisingly large numbers of people with this close but extremely partial acquaintance with Christian missions.

Others, again, became Christians. But the church has been mainly among the poor and ignorant, and the rank and file of the ministry not such as are able to attract and hold educated young people; moreover, the schools and colleges have been dominated for the most part by a highly liberal version of Protestantism, while the churches have been mainly fundamentalist. Few educated young people have found a permanent and satisfying home in the church. They have tended rather to drift into the "Christian movement." A man retained the Christian name, but with a steadily decreasing Christian content, because he was outside the corporate life and discipline of a Christian community. In the end, much more often than not, he ceased to be effectively a Christian at all. The larger cities were full of ex-Christians of this kind, among them a large proportion of those Christians in high positions in the Kuomintang Government of Chiang Kai-shek who were so much praised in the West a few years ago.

The "Christian movement" did, however, also provide a haven

for some of those serious Christians who were unwilling to accept missionary leadership, missionary ideas, and what I think must be called "missionary sterility" (a disease that attacked the Chinese leaders we have trained as much as it attacked us). It is significant that these men are now returning to the church and are the leaders of the Chinese theological movement that is just beginning. One cause of all this is their perception of the futile superficiality of the humanist versions of the "social gospel" to which they had earlier given their allegiance. But there are other reasons, among them undoubtedly the realization that the Chinese church now belongs to Chinese, and patriotic Chinese can gladly belong to it. In them the Christian movement has found a partial justification.

Last of all, some of the most zealous Christians among the alumni of our schools have joined and become leaders in the indigenous sects, which are nationalist, in reaction against missionaries, and pentecostalist and millenarist, in reaction against the sterility of the church and the badness of the times.

Whether they are viewed from the angle of their creative contribution to the needs of Chinese society or of their provision of leadership from the Chinese church, the educational institutions on which we have lavished so much time, money, and loving hard work therefore seem for the most part to have made a poor return.

The case of the hospitals is not substantially different. They have, of course, healed very large numbers. But they have not created a Chinese medical profession with a conception of its task relevant to Chinese conditions, nor have they been an effective sign of the Christian passion that men and women should have wholeness of life. We attempted, as we were able, to create in China hospitals and medical and nursing schools that would not be wholly unworthy of the institutions in the West at which medical missionaries were themselves trained. Their products have been accustomed to at least the more essential of the Western medical equipment, and have been unwilling to leave the few large cities where these were available; and they have not been insensitive to the delights of the Western-style middle-class life which their missionary teachers enjoyed and which is impossible outside the large cities.

Medically speaking, however, the real need of China is for basic work in public health, the control of epidemics, and the reduction of malnutrition — a program requiring much larger numbers of workers, with a substantially lower standard of training, stationed in villages and market towns all over the country. This is the program of the Communists, not of the Christians. The public health program of the church hospitals, when there has been one, has too often been centered upon the hospital; and to be effective outside a narrow radius has required vast expenditure of foreign money on transportation.

Religiously, the hospitals have been somewhat of a danger to the church because of the immense economic power of the leading Christian doctors and nurses by contrast with the rank and file of the church membership. Since costs in China have risen steeply, and mission subsidies declined in volume and still more in purchasing power, they have been forced to raise their fees. The amount of free or very cheap treatments given has been sharply reduced, and they have tended to become institutions with a better standard than those supported by the government, but charging fees that only the well-to-do can pay. The result is that, like the schools, they have in effect taken their place in Chinese bourgeois society (to translate *compradore* class very roughly into a more familiar term).

This picture is doubtless somewhat overdrawn for emphasis; any missionary could point to exceptions in his own experience. As the writer reflects on *his* own experience — chairman of a hospital board of managers, secretary of a college board of managers, and concerned with several schools and another hospital — he cannot feel that it is more than the modest exaggeration of a real truth. That in the course of all this much good was done is obvious. What cannot be denied in his experience is the lack of a creative Christian purpose, planted deep both in the gospel and in the soil of China, in the work of all these people, this money, this time, this devotion. And can a China missionary be free of the fear that what was true of China is true still of India and Africa?

The rock on which the much smaller amount of rural service work foundered was also the revolution, but in a different way. We sought to spread knowledge of improved strains of rice, wheat, vegetables, chickens, and the like, and improved methods of cultivation and care; to promote literacy and public health; and to foster a self-supporting rural church. These aims were revolutionary aims in the landlord-dominated society of the Chinese countryside, which was as static as the landlords could keep it. They could only achieve success if the power of the landlords was destroyed or curtailed; and the landlords were the principal class upon which the Kuomintang government of General Chiang Kai-shek rested. Our rural service work prospered, therefore, in a merely superficial sense; for it never made fruitful contact with the moving forces in Chinese society. Such effectiveness as it enjoyed depended upon plenty of foreign help.

It is therefore incontestable that our institutional work, for all its valuable by-products, failed to be socially creative. We failed to take seriously the fact that Chinese society was ripe for revolution — to take seriously the very fact which the Communists understood so thoroughly and to understanding and meeting which they owe their success. Why did we so fail? The Communist answer will be, "Because of your bourgeois capitalist background"; and this is a crude but true way of stating the facts. Our own reply would perhaps be "Because we were not trained in economics and sociology"; but behind that lack lies the feeling that economics and sociology are not truly important to a gospel minister, and the fear that most of us surely have of revolution itself, of the Chinese masses taking initiative into their own hands. That is precisely the sort of thing that Communists mean when they talk about our "bourgeois capitalist background." It may be argued that social creativity is no part, or not a main part, of the Christian missionary task. Such a view has not been accepted by the main missionary societies; for they have included the rebuilding of society as a part of the wholeness and fullness that the Gospel seeks to offer. Our failure is therefore major, not minor.

To turn now to our religious failure, we may begin with some words of Roland Allen's:

> We have allowed racial and religious pride to direct our attitude towards those whom we have been wont to call 'poor heathen.' We have approached them as superior beings, moved by charity to impart of our wealth to destitute and perishing souls. We have used that argument at home to wring grudging and pitiful doles for the propagation of our faith, and abroad we have adopted

that attitude as missionaries of a superior religion. We have not learnt the lesson that it is not for our righteousness that we have been entrusted with the Gospel, but that we may be instruments in God's hands for revealing the universal salvation of His Son in all the world. We have not learnt that as Christians we exist by the Spirit of Him who gave up the glory of Heaven in order to pour out His life for the redemption of the world. We have not learnt the lesson that our own hope, our own salvation, our own glory, lies in the completion of the Temple of the Lord. We have not understood that the members of the Body of Christ are scattered in all lands, and that we, without them, are not made perfect. We have thought of the Temple of the Lord as complete in us, of the Body of Christ as consisting of us, and we have thought of the heathen as the extension of the body of which we are the members. Consequently, we have preached the Gospel from the point of view of the wealthy man who casts a mite into the lap of the beggar, rather than from the point of view of the husbandman who casts his seed into the earth, knowing that his own life and the lives of all connected with him depend upon the crop which will result from his labour.

Approaching them in that spirit, we have desired to help them. We have been anxious to do something for them. And we have done much. We have done everything for them. We have taught them, baptised them, shepherded them. We have managed their funds, ordered their services, built their churches, provided their teachers. We have nursed them, fed them, doctored them. We have trained them, and have even ordained some of them. We have done everything for them, but very little with them. We have done everything for them except give place to them. We have treated them as 'dear children', but not as 'brethren.'

(*Missionary Methods,* 1912)

That was written forty years ago; and it is, of course, no longer a true picture of the church and the mission in China. But although there are few of whom that is now true, there are probably none of us in whom there is no trace of that attitude. Although we have dropped that crude pride, we have not yet, and our supporters at home have not yet, understood the positive Christian truth that renders it intolerable. How many can say that Chinese, Indian, African, Japanese, Fiji, Melanesian and the other Christians are essential to us — that without them we shall not be made perfect — and as they say it, know that they are saying something that is vital to their own church life? Moreover, many Chinese, and still more Indians and Africans, believe that Allen's account of the matter is the true one, and that if we have changed our ways, it is mainly due to factors outside our control, three in number. The first is political: the main reason why the transference of control from missionary to national occurred in China earlier than in India (though the church in China is both younger and smaller than in India) is that China had its first nationalist revolution as long ago as 1927; the new government required that all school principals be Chinese, and where schools led the way, other departments of church life followed, slowly. The second is economic: the worldwide depression that began in 1928 cut the numbers of missionaries and the amount of their funds drastically, and immensely speeded up the process of self-support and the replacement of foreign missionaries by nationals; it also meant that missionaries disposed of less money and encouraged a different attitude among them and among others to them. The third is cultural: we are less sure of our superiority. These things have begun among us a change of heart. It is said, but I think it must be acknowledged, that the initiative, save in rare souls, came from outside the church. If some of us see these things with a new clarity, we have to admit that we should have taken much longer to see them, and might never have seen them at all, if a Communist revolution that resulted in our departure had not caused us to reflect on our works and our faith with a self-critical attitude for which normally we found neither time nor courage.

In this light, let us survey rapidly the issues that do now divide foreign missionaries from Christian nationals. First, in the world as a whole, though not in China, is racial prejudice and the color bar to which it gives rise. (This kind of thing used to be found also in China.) The core of the race problem is the mixed marriage, and we have to be clear what we think about that. Chinese generally are not much interested in the subject, but they are aware of the Western prejudices. I have often been exhaustively questioned by Chinese friends on my attitude. What I think they sought to discover was whether an apparently unprejudiced young foreigner was in fact sound or not. We can take it absolutely for granted that there is an immense amount of justified suspicion on this score, which includes all the British and is not confined to South Africans and to the white inhabitants of the southern states in the U.S.A.; and that any compromise will be bitterly resented, however justifiable it may seem to us. The place for most of us to start is not to demand broader attitudes among missionaries or other white men overseas, but to ensure that the many Africans and others from overseas who come here to study or work are made to feel at home, which not infrequently means being invited into your home and mine.

The second issue — first in China — is money; and that in two forms: the control over mission and church finances, and the comparative wealth of the missionary by contrast with the poverty of the Chinese church worker. The maxim "He who pays the piper calls the tune" is not included in the New Testament, but it is widely acted upon by Christians. Even in these last years, the relatively impoverished British missionary (to say nothing of his American colleague handling those world-coveted U.S. dollars) has been relatively a source of wealth: his analogue is the rice Christian, the man who hangs around the missionary for what he can get out of him. Mission funds were, until a year or two ago, a large part of the budget of any diocese: it was impossible for Chinese not to pay undue attention to the missionary because inevitably they felt that his opinion might be important at home; and in China his opinion acquired for this reason an importance that might be spurious. More serious than all this, however, was the fact that even in advanced dioceses, which were perhaps 80 percent self-supporting, an unsatisfactory and debilitating equilibrium had been reached. We were mainly, but not wholly, self-supporting. We had made great efforts and were aware of it. There seemed — short of the intervention from outside that finally came upon us — no reason why we should ever become fully independent. This uneasy equilibrium had disastrous spiritual results: Chinese were aware of their dependence and resented it (and us); but they could not face doing without our help, nor take the risk of wholly ignoring our opinions.

The question of standards and manners of living was worse still. The writer was paid about three times as much as a Chinese of comparable age and responsibility in the church; and there were comparable missionaries of other missions paid three times as much as he. Chinese friends were good enough to consider that the latter was the more significant difference. But it is the former that counts. It is very difficult to get this problem into perspective and to avoid both sentimentality and hard-heartedness; but it is very important to do so, because too many missionaries have had a guilty conscience for years, and a guilty conscience is inhibiting and frustrating.

The existence of radically different standards and manners of life is a stumbling-block because it creates a middle wall of partition that limits, cramps, or destroys free fellowship between Christians. At least in the big cities, where of recent years most missionaries have worked, it was only fairly Westernized Chinese who could feel really at home in our houses, however simply we lived by our standards. Many Western adults, and still more children, cannot live on Chinese food, in the Chinese way, or on the Chinese professional person's income. It can be done most easily where modern methods of hygiene and public health are available and understood and used by national as well as foreign members of some community or institution; and experiments of this sort of simple village living by missionary families may be able to avoid the appalling death rate among children in the past to which the foreign cemeteries in China bear mute witness. Those who have in one way or another "lived Chinese" know what an immense difference it makes to live in the same way, in the same context, sharing many of one's leisure hours in the came conversation and amusements, with one's Chinese colleagues. But living Chinese is hard, and may often be impossible, for families.

There are those who hold that living standards are not the key: that the key is spiritual attitude. Formally, of course, this is true. Christians do not always do justice to the extent to which how one lives will, in fact, condition, if it does not determine, what one feels, and so become truly guilty of the error the Marxists call "idealism." The other false escape from the dilemma is in effect to sacrifice the family to the gospel: one mission in China is said to have been almost proud of the fact that its frontier advanced upon the bodies of women and children. Surely at the roots of such a view is heresy. A vocation to marriage is a vocation to glorify God in a particular state with its necessary rights and duties. It can only be combined with the vocation of a pioneer missionary of the classic type if matrimony is felt to be spiritually neutral, irrelevant to God's calling. Marriage can only be irrelevant if we believe that the body, matter, is neutral, irrelevant, or evil. Men cannot believe that and believe the Christian faith. God made matter and was incarnate in it: the comparison of the relation of husband and wife to that between Christ and the church naturally follows. But this conclusion is not always drawn, for orthodox Christians are often prone to speak and behave as if the Word, as it were, became not flesh, but spirit. The flesh — matter generally — must be given its due: not more than its due, but not less. On both of these issues, the imminence of Marxism may usefully cause us to be careful about Christian truth.

The conclusion is that where manner of life constitutes a bar to full fellowship, manner of life must be altered, and that on the evidence, we should be chary of a facile assumption that differing manners of life do not create such barriers. It is therefore not accidental that the large majority of missionaries are already single women — celibates, though not all would use that term. If missionary service becomes virtually a celibate vocation, and if all of us conform our manner of life to the simplest up-country standards, there will be a considerably increased wastage rate from missionaries retiring early on grounds of health. (The wastage rate in the early nineteenth century was, of course, very high indeed.)

The conclusion that the answer is celibacy and austerity, which has behind it the massive experience of Rome and the opinion of at least one missionary thinker who is neither celibate nor Roman, has been contested. Experiment will decide. It cannot be contested that in conventional missionary life real barriers are set up, and that this circumstance is eating away at the respect for the spiritual authority of the missionary which Christian nationals may rightly feel. (There is a proper respect to be accorded to anyone with a commission from God, quite different from the false and improper sorts of respect that money or foreigners have formerly conferred, and that have indeed been easily destroyed by them.) It is eating

away also at the assurance, in the evangelical sense, that even a
sinful missionary ought to have. A sense of sin forgiven is one thing:
a guilty conscience about a problem that is recognized but not
faced and overcome is quite another.

This list is doubtless not exhaustive; but it is time to turn to
a range of problems that has already been hinted at; and here again
we quote from Roland Allen:

> In our organisation missionaries are a professional class. Chris-
> tians leave our shores in great numbers: few are, or think them-
> selves to be, or think that they ought to be, missionaries of the
> gospel. We do not expect that where they go the heathen will
> be converted and churches established spontaneously. It is almost
> universally taken for granted that missionary work is the work of
> a paid professional class, and that the utmost that can be expected
> of those who do not belong to this class is to support those who
> do; and even that is not expected of the majority. Missionary
> societies began their crusade not by striving to call out the spirit
> of Christian men whose occupation carried them abroad, not by
> trying to impress upon the Church at home that Christ calls all
> His people to witness for Him wherever they may be, wherever
> they may go, but by creating an army of professional missionaries.
> The whole system of secretaries, boards, offices, accounts, con-
> tracts with missionaries, statistical returns, reports, reeks of it.
> From every missionary society there goes out every day and into
> every part of the world with one insistent unceasing voice, the
> proclamation that the Gospel must be preached in all the world,
> and that it must be preached by special agents maintained by a
> society for this particular work. No verbal denials can shake it. . . .
>   . . . The conception of the Church, held both by the Epis-
> copacy at home and by the leaders of the societies, was identical.
> They were far removed from the Apostolic Church: the only
> Church organisation with which they were familiar was the or-
> ganisation of a national Church, in a country which had for
> centuries been nominally Christian. They thought of bishops as
> great officials governing and directing, more or less, large num-
> bers of clergy, most of whom they scarcely knew by sight, in
> dioceses so large that they could not possibly visit the parishes

except at rare intervals. They thought of parish priests as officials of the Church who ruled almost autocratically in their parishes responsible not at all to the laity for their conduct, and only partially to their bishops. They thought of the laity not so much as members of the Church but as people whose duty it was to obey the Church as represented by her bishops and priests. The apostolic conception of the bishop as the father of a Spiritual Family, as the Pastor of a flock every member of which he should know by name was lost. Men still used the titles 'Chief Pastor' and 'Father of God'; but they did not expect him to know his family, or his flock, personally and intimately. Both bishop and priest were officials, and paid officials, separated widely from the laity by training and by conventional manners and customs.

(*Spontaneous Expansion of the Church,* 1927)

This paralyzing professional clericalism, which we have exported so faithfully to the mission field, is perhaps a product of the evangelization of Europe in the Dark Ages mainly by monks, with secular rulers leading their people — not without effective pressures — *en masse* into the faith: some authorities consider that we may never have recovered from these purely nominally Christian masses. However that may be, we are cursed with precisely the disease on which in these passages Allen laid his finger, even if, in the twenty years since his *Spontaneous Expansion* was published, we have made some progress.

The result, at all events, is evident: it is sterility. Immense energies are occupied, as they are in England, by simply keeping things going; if the ecclesiastical organization in England is out of date and irrelevant, how much more so in China. There is some passivity on the part of the large bulk of the laity — though to a degree not as intense as with us at home.

But much more serious than these things is the deformation of church life that results from our practice in regard to the ministry and the sacraments. In one diocese known to the writer, not worse starved than most, we had about two hundred and fifty congregations and about thirty-five clergy. These were not all available for ordinary parish work. The twenty-five to thirty or so who were available were moved around with considerable frequency in an attempt to stop the worst gaps. They did not belong to their people and were not habitually popular with or respected by them. Our conception of the priesthood was ideally a sort of cross between Richard Baxter and George Herbert, the conception that has dominated Anglicanism in Britain since the seventeenth century, not wholly without reason. It is proving a disadvantage today in England: it is disastrously irrelevant in China. There are a few such people available, and they make first-class leaders; but to attempt to provide sufficient clergy for a relatively large and growing diocese in that way is to ask the impossible. You have to eke it out with pious mice and the unworthy — and even then are woefully short. In the same way, one Bishop attempted to itinerate for Confirmations and pastoral oversight among these two hundred and fifty congregations; and the task was impossible. Everywhere there were people who had been prepared for Confirmation but could not be confirmed, and people longing for the Eucharist and unable to receive it for lack of a priest to celebrate.

The inevitable result followed. A sacramental system that is exalted but practically unusable falls into contempt. The indigenous sects already referred to spread their influence. If your own church cannot provide you with an effective ministry and frequent sacraments, and is not organized, whatever its formal theology, in such a way that you feel you are a member of a spiritual fellowship, you will (if you mean business) more often than not join some other that can provide these blessings, whatever its other failings. One of the most widely spread of these sects has, in the manner of the Plymouth Brethren, a breaking of bread for believers each Sunday and is both a real and an expanding fellowship.

It is a tragedy that catholic order and the freedom of the Spirit were ever opposed to each other; and it would not have happened if we had not exported to China our own torn and mutilated Western post-medieval Christian tradition. The sects are now heretical, and likely to grow more so: this is because they began as protests against our errors. Allen maintains that where missionaries come into contact for the first time with groups who have learned the gospel from relatively ignorant and untrained Chinese, it is found that what they have learned they have learned both truly and deeply, and that they are anxious for more. He makes the further point that in the early church the source of heresies was not the inrush of more or less illiterate converts (the prospect of which so disturbs us), but the speculations of learned men.

At all events, for these major and other minor contributory reasons, we were marked by a dull sterility, a preoccupation with matters that were, by any serious standard, of secondary and tertiary importance. At home, for that matter, many of the clergy are laboring under the same disability. It was due to our having taken with us not only the gospel (with that basic order which is, of course, a part of it), but a theological construction in which the gospel was imprisoned; the church owed more to all sorts of irrelevant historical factors than to theology proper.

This leads me to a final point: our theological failure. Theology never had a chance in China, for various local reasons. But almost all the younger churches seem to be theologically sterile, so this cannot be due to local Chinese factors. It is surely due to our habit of assuming that to attain positions of leadership, Chinese must follow Christian doctrine as it developed in the Jewish-Greek world of the early church, the Latin medieval world, and the Anglo-Saxon world of the Reformation and later. And this, in turn, is due to a more disastrous assumption still: that theology and Christian morals were both to be taken upon the missionary's authority. Few things in Allen's writings are more impressive than his contrast between our handling of the intellectual issues of the faith and St. Paul's. The result is that the correct answers have been learned, but the reasons for them have never entered deeply into men's Christian lives because they did not in the first instance spring out of them. Much of the writer's time was happily spent in the teaching of church history and historical theology, and there are few more important subjects for a younger church; but they are useless studies until the student has encountered in himself and his church the questions to which the classical theological controversialists were seeking the answers. An ignorant young foreigner was trying to formulate the living issues in the church in China (about which he really knew extremely little) in order that his students might recognize that the substance of their studies was of serious value to them. He only succeeded with those few who had sufficient depth and independence to have reflected already for themselves upon the nature of the common life in the body of Christ as they knew it in the church. And this in turn was mainly due — for theological students in China have a much closer relation to the parochial life of the church than is common in the West — to the fact that in day-to-day church life neither the people nor the parson had been taught to think issues out for themselves from first principles as St. Paul, and for that matter St. Peter, taught his people to do.

Since we have never thought through our own problems theologically — asking always the question, "What are we really trying to do?" — and therefore never fostered that habit among the Chinese, the faith never acquired a truly Chinese expression. There are Chinese intellectuals: most of them have no theology worth speaking of; and what they have is seriously, not to say appallingly, heretical. There are orthodox Christians: they are mostly simple-minded fundamentalists, or educated clergy whose thought is not at bottom their own or Chinese, but remains woodenly in Western categories. There is a vacuum. It has been filled mainly by dialectical materialism. If today there are signs of the beginning of a Chinese theological movement, it is due principally to the realization, tragically belated, that Marxism must be encountered and mastered.

The right word to describe what has happened to Christian missions in China is "débâcle."

(So far as I know, this verdict was first passed in an article in the *International Review of Missions* for October, 1951 [to which these pages are greatly in debt]. The article appears to have been widely regretted. It is objected that the missionary era would have come to an end in China anyway: had we all been wise as serpents and harmless as doves, had all the lessons we are now learning been applied years ago, we would probably still have been eliminated. It is unquestionably true that in the last few years our attitudes have not mattered: the end of the missionary era resulted from purely political forces, rooted in the Communist understanding of the world today. On the longer issue, I am not so sure. We do not know what would have been the result of St. Paul's methods in China: perhaps he would have captured the Taiping movements. We do not know.

But the historical judgment is not the point. The term *débâcle* expresses the judgment [in theological language, not historical but eschatological] that God found us wanting. There is no way of proving these things. I can only bear my own witness to the fact that in my own experience [which has given me a wide range of friendships among Chinese and missionaries of many traditions] the best of us left China sadly, with many happy memories, but with a sense that the Communists had cut a series of Gordian knots with which we had wrestled in vain because — because in the final analysis we were wrong. A radical sense of the judgment of God, which had begun to work in me earlier, has since then dominated my attempt to understand what happened. I have attempted to put this as clearly as I can in the first chapter, and it is this, and not my *obiter dicta* on mission policy, which seems to me at least, to be important. To say these things gives pain to some people and suggests to others that we were unhappy or frustrated or are depressed or neurotic. I deeply regret the first consequence; the others are, to the best of my belief, untrue.)

The practical reasons for the ending of the missionary era in China are of course external to the church and the mission; they are political. But in the months between the realization that we should be leaving much earlier than we thought and our actual departure, months in which we had unaccustomed leisure and every opportunity for thoughtful self-examination, it became evident to some of us, and to many more of our Chinese friends, that our mandate had been withdrawn; that the time for missions as we had known them had passed; that the end of the missionary era was the will of God.

I met in a bus the other day an African priest from Nigeria. He introduced himself, and we got talking. As I explained to him in outline some of these things, his initial politeness about "one of the missionary heroes from China" disappeared; and he began to say how like Nigeria was to China.

Let us avoid misunderstanding if we can. There is nothing here to give anyone an excuse for evading a share in the world mission of the church. But the conclusion must stand that the foreign mission that the writer has known and has been in a very small measure responsible for, is now not only out of date, but was in important respects wrongly conceived. Fortunately there are other possibilities open to us, which the débâcle in China itself may make us the more ready to explore. This may be added: it is not only in China, or generally among the younger churches, that the work of the church is conceived and carried out on wrong or out-of-date lines; and there are more signs in the younger churches than in the older of the necessary reformation under the Word of God.

III. Looking Ahead

In the decades before the Second World War, missionaries grew accustomed to a freedom of action possessed neither by their predecessors who began the work nor by ourselves today. There were, of course, limitations upon this freedom, imposed internally by shortage of funds and of recruits, and externally by governments, and latterly also by the need — or, more accurately, the desirability — to take into account the opinions of Christian nationals. But there was a substantial freedom of action and a sense of leisure, of time available, which made planning possible. Even after the Second World War we behaved as if this were still true in China. Much of our work of reconstruction and rehabilitation after the devastation of the war assumed that we had at least a decade or two: commonly, the first missionaries returned in 1946; and the last had ceased work by 1952.

China is but an extreme example of a general trend. Within the mission and the church we are short of money and people; without, we work in a world that is increasingly dominated by nationalist governments and nationalist sentiments and by the worldwide trend towards the assumption by governments of ever-increasing responsibility for all sides of life. Even where no liberation has taken place, where there is no immediate prospect of a diplomatic break with Britain or America, governments are themselves increasingly active in education and medicine; and they lay down

85

ever stricter regulations affecting churches and missions. And in those same areas, there is a steadily mounting pressure upon the mission from the leaders of the church that policy shall be what they desire and not what we think best. The persisting façade of Western bishops and Western leaders conceals a potentially explosive situation and results not merely in the restriction or even extinction of freedom of action, but too often in a state of paralysis. We not only cannot do what we want to do, but not infrequently cannot decide what it is we want to do.

In some ways this is a temporary situation, characteristic of the uneasy transition from control by the mission and by the missionaries to control by the church and by nationals. As we seek to understand our own missionary responsibility in this period, we shall remember that we are seeking, so far as it is in our power to do so, the best conditions for the church that will before long be wholly responsible. We shall therefore be wise to assume that, in the foreseeable future, there will not be either for the present or the later leadership of the church that freedom of action to which we have been accustomed.

In the period immediately after the liberation of China, we tended to assume that if we could clear up some of the outstanding messes, the authorities would welcome the contribution of the church and the mission as long as it took into account the general policies of the People's Government. This was a mistake, and a mistake from which a clearer understanding of Marxism should have delivered us. In Marxist theory, the people, under the leadership of the Communist Party, alone understand the needs of the country. The assumption of independent initiative by sectional interests cannot but be undesirable: if the policies which such interests desire to forward are right, they will be already included in the policies of the People's Government; if they are not so included, this can only be because they are undesirable (probably because they are counterrevolutionary, feudalistic, or subservient to the interests of imperialism). There can be — as a matter of dogmatic conviction — no desirable, independent initiative at all. The course for private bodies to pursue is to accept wholeheartedly the general policies of the People's Government, and to cooperate in such specific matters as may be suggested to them by the People's Government.

We may expect that this rigorous conviction will not everywhere be dominant, but we must expect to meet everywhere this sort of approach rather than the liberal atmosphere to which we have been accustomed in the capitalist democratic West.

That is one overriding element in the future setting of the mission. Its corollary is the shortness of time. A responsible missionary society secretary has been heard to say that he thought all missionaries would be out of West Africa in five years' time. It is true that he is a China man, and may have been unduly affected by events in China. Another leading missionary remarked that before long Congress will be succeeded by the Hindu Mahasabha, and the Mahasabha in turn by the Communist liberation of India: "How long do you think this will take?" "Oh, about five years." It is true that he takes a more revolutionary view of Indian policies than most missionaries, but that of itself does not make him wrong.

We should be well advised, therefore, to take it for granted that the time is short. This is true even if you think — like some American extremists — that we can and should destroy Communism before it becomes strong enough to destroy us. The hope of eliminating what we call Communism from the world seems as little likely of achievement as the seventeenth century hopes that Protestant would destroy Catholic or vice versa. Even if we did so, we should not return to the bourgeois world or recreate a paradise for well-to-do, powerful, and benevolent Anglo-Saxons. The restrictions alike on Anglo-Saxon power and on Anglo-Saxon benevolence remain, and indeed are increasing. This time, in fact, is short.

This leads some people to think that missions, and indeed any Western activity in Asia and Africa, are not worthwhile. There still remains with us the assumption that if we can't plan for decades ahead, if it is unreasonable to hope that we can start something that will grow a fine old tradition and gather round it the affections of a dozen parishes and half a dozen Sunday schools, then we had better pack up. But that kind of response is wrong, both practically and religiously. Religiously it is surely true, as Chancellor T. R. Milford has said, "that Christians must learn again what Christians have always known, how to live without immediate hopes in the world." (I may observe in passing that this is not contradictory of what we said in the first chapter about the Christian hope; for after all, we hope in God and not in the permanence of our good works. The devils are subject unto us, but the important thing is that our names are written in heaven.) To live without immediate hope means that we get on with the immediate job that is given to us, seeking indeed to understand it in what, so far as we can see, is likely to be its setting — understanding all we can of the signs of the times — but leaving the issue in God's hand. All of us are today like Abraham, going up from Harran, but not knowing where we go and what in the long run we are to do. "I do not ask to see the distant scene: one step enough for me." Moreover, a radical pessimism is also practically unnecessary. A man can do a very great deal in five years — if those years are well and shrewdly and devotedly spent — a big "if." But if we act upon the right assumptions, there is no end to the things that God might do in us; and of course we may get longer than now seems likely.

What then shall we say positively of the purpose of missions? There would perhaps be general agreement with a statement on the following lines:

The work of missions is the planting of the visible church in all its completeness in areas where it has never existed or has now ceased to exist. This may also be expressed by saying that missions have as their aim the growth of the church to its divinely appointed limits, which are identical with the geographical distribution of the human race. The mission field is, in fact, those countries where the visible church is not securely planted, together with those sections of the population of a country otherwise part of Christendom that are left untouched by the church of that country, as, for example, Moslems in Yugoslavia, and — so the leaders of the *Mission de Paris* would say — the proletariat in the West. The visible church may be said to be planted when she is sufficiently stable to recruit her clergy from her own country and not require to rely on foreigners; when she has shown her ability to spread beyond a clique or a social class; when her work is affecting, if only in small degree, the whole range of the life of the country; and when there is sufficient organization to permit unity of discipline.

There are some corollaries of this statement that may not at first sight command such ready agreement. The aim of missions is not primarily to save souls, but to provide the permanent means by which souls may be saved. In Christendom this provision has been made, even if it is badly handled and genuinely neglected; in the mission field, it has not. Secondly, although souls must be saved until the last day, it is not certain that missionary work so defined will continue to the last day. This specifically missionary task thus understood is transitory; it is completed when the church is established throughout the world. The mission of the church to the world, of course, continues. Thirdly, anyone is a missionary who is engaged upon this work, whether he is a national of the country or a foreigner. The missionary is defined by his task, not by his nationality. Fourthly, the provision of the sacraments for all is essential: a national ministry must be provided as soon as possible.

"Instead of saying, 'Let us first make numerous Christians in order to obtain a full native ministry,' we should reverse our terms and say: 'Let us first make a vigorous native ministry in order to obtain numerous Christians.' " This is a Roman Catholic statement, but the Roman origin is not very obvious. Much more obvious is the way in which it summarizes and illuminates so much of our own experience. One of the reasons for which it is permissible to hope for a wider occasional study of Roman writings on the part of the rest of us is that the very systematic, not to say formal, method of their thought — the very thing that is often so offensive and boring to us — can at times be of great value to us.

There is one school of thought and practice among us, however, that would reject the center of Père Charles's teaching. The recent emphasis of almost all of the main mission societies has been upon the planting of the church. There are some societies, however, and a great many small groups and individuals, who in practice, at all events, would ignore, minimize, or reject it. (One such body only in the last decade revised its articles of association to include the aim of planting the church.) The results of the policy of preaching the gospel as extensively as possible, but not giving any time to the planting and organization of the church, become evident when foreign missionaries have to leave. Not much remains.

But if we are thoroughly committed in practice as well as in theory to the aim of planting a church and to the conviction that the missionary task proper is a transitory one, certain disconcerting conclusions follow.

There has been everywhere, since the Tambaram Conference of the International Missionary Council in 1938, an emphasis on the importance of the ministry. It is, however, doubtful whether we have yet absorbed the implications for the life of the church of the revival of biblical theology, perhaps because we have not yet shaken off some of our own historical trappings.

Mr. Allen quotes Father Herbert Kelly (founder of the Society of the Sacred Mission at Kelham):

> Let us imagine ourselves in some small primitive church met to choose a pastor. Our course is quite obvious. Normally, we want an experienced, middle-aged Christian of strong character and independent position, who is not and need not be afraid to speak to us, a man zealous for his faith and who understands it, learned in the Scriptures. We have no college-trained men among us, but at forty a man has learnt from life. We are not trying young experiments. We want someone to lead us and help us such as we are, and we all know one another's minds and capacities much better than a board of examiners will ever do. . . . If the village chooses one of its own members, no (financial) difficulty arises; he is already providing for himself, and is in position to go on doing so, no doubt with some assistance of gifts in money, kind, or labour to compensate for any loss of time through his pastoral labours. . . . The village-farmer priest is the father of a family. Of course, being a priest he is a priest in the Catholic Church, but this does not mean he is not free to accept 'a call' wherever sufficient inducement offers. He is ordained to his own people. . . . That is a sufficient ministry which supplies what the Church really needs at the time. When the needs of the Church become more complex, the ministry will naturally be elaborated to meet them. . . . [In the early Church] in the cities quite at the beginning, the system was the same as in the country, . . . but the growing mass of Church business gave rise to the minor orders . . . and provided an opening for young men who might like to devote their life to the clerical profession. . . . In the towns the bishop was normally though not necessarily chosen from the

professional clergy. This professionalism was not regarded as fundamental. It grew up where it was wanted, and the business which called it into being provided the means for its support.

(*Spontaneous Expansion of the Church*, 1927)

Mr. Allen would add that in order to make sure that the Eucharist could always be celebrated and that other functions of the priest — such as teaching and preaching — did not prove a strain, we should ordain not one such village farmer priest, but a college of them, and thus conform still more closely to the Pauline practice. This is precisely what is needed generally in the younger churches. And the best men — those we see, for example, over in this country — in the professional ministry would be required, as they were in the early church, to deal with the "growing mass of Church business" which will remain even if the unnecessary complexities introduced by the mission are removed.

This is so sensible, so biblical, so catholic, so admirably suited to the needs of the younger churches, and indeed, in face of the increasing shortage of the clergy, and in the increasing financial crisis of the older churches too, that it is exceedingly difficult to understand why we are so reluctant to act upon it. The answer seems to be that we have never recovered from the Middle Ages. In the back of our minds always is the Mass priest and his ignorant, superstitious, passive laity. In the inevitable, desirable, tragic upheaval of the Reformation, things were sundered that God had joined together; in his mercy, God is bringing them together again as we all return to the theology of the Bible in the setting of the ecumenical movement, seeking to recover not only the unity, but also the wholeness and renewal of the church.

The Anglican parson, suspicious of lay initiative; the Anglican layman, at once demanding a parson to give a lead and doubtful of, or bored by, the sort of lead he gives; the Free Churchman, obsessed by the fear of "prelacy," and because this has led him to reject or distort catholic order, suffering the deformation of the life of the body of Christ into a caricature of parliamentary democracy — it is not surprising that without distinction of denomination, we have lost the secret of "spontaneous expansion of the church."

Before we leave this subject, let us hear some final words from
Roland Allen, writing of a missionary who proceeded upon other
than the usual lines:

Soon the missionary learnt that the secret of success in his work
lay in dealing with the Church as a body. When questions arose
he had but one answer: 'Tell it to the Church'. A man came to
him one day with a long tale of persecution. . . . The only answer
that he received was, 'Tell it to the Church'. Eventually he did
so. . . . Then an old farmer arose in the congregation and asked,
'Has your adversary taken the case to court?' 'No but he threatens
to do so'. 'Then I propose that we adjourn this matter until he
carries out his threat'. . . . Some weeks later the same man came
to say that his enemy had now taken the case to court and to
appeal for help. Again, an old man arose: 'I think that we had
better not consider this matter any more'. Again the sentence
was received in silence. In that silence the whole Church had
condemned their brother. . . . A question which might have
perplexed and troubled a foreigner, one in which he might easily
have made a serious mistake, was settled. No Christian in the
congregation would have dared to tell a foreign priest that the
man was wrong . . . but none need break the silence of condem-
nation. . . . The aged, respectable leader, illiterate, ignorant in
many ways, dull though he might be, in the council of the Church
found his voice and fulfilled a duty which would have tried the
wisdom of the best educated and best instructed teacher.
    Very soon the Church began to realize itself. Sunday by
Sunday the congregation sat discussing questions of a church
order, of instructing one another in the faith. Most often the
missionary himself could not be present. . . . He was not afraid
that they would make serious mistakes or take hasty action behind
his back. The more he retired from them, the more they turned
to him in case of need, the more they sought his advice, the
more they told him their plans, the more they saved him from
difficulties. . . . One day (the catechist) came into the missionary's house with a question: Do you know what you are doing,
Sir? . . . If you go on like this, you will found a native Church.
                                                    (*Missionary Methods*)

And again:

> What then ought the missionary to do? If he has baptised the
> first converts, we may take it for granted that he has assured
> himself that they are in the Faith, and he ought then to invite
> the Bishop to act towards them as the Apostles and their imme-
> diate followers acted in like case. . . . The Bishop must deliver
> to them what St. Paul called 'the tradition' (of which the Apos-
> tles' Creed is the later expression) that they may have a standard
> by which to try all that they may hear later. The Creed is a
> touchstone. . . . When each has heard it (and it may be expressed
> in very simple language so that the most ignorant can really *hear*
> it) he must be prepared to say, 'That I believe: That is my
> belief'. . . . Thereafter it is theirs. It belongs to them as much
> as it belongs to us. The Bishop must deliver to them the Gospel,
> that they know where to turn for instruction. For they must learn
> from the very beginning to rely upon God, not upon men; upon
> the Bible, not upon human teachers. Here again, when he
> delivers the Bible to the Church, it does not follow that every
> member of the congregation must be able to read it; but it does
> follow that all the Christians must learn to revere it and to know
> it. . . . The Sacraments must be delivered to the Church. The
> Bishop must make sure that they have learnt the manner and the
> meaning of their observance. They must be taught how to ad-
> minister them, and how to receive them, practically. . . . I have
> a profound belief in the power of the Sacraments. I believe that
> in a Divine way the use of them teaches the teachable their inward
> meaning . . . and therefore I think we need to be in no hurry
> to attempt to teach new converts all that we think we know about
> them. . . . Ministers must be ordained that the Church may have
> a Christian government and officers to direct the proper conduct
> of the Church and the due administration of her rites. . . . Here
> again it is the Church as a whole which receives officers, not
> officers which receive a Church . . . and the Church as a whole
> should be responsible for the good conduct of the Church. . . .
> The Bishop should tell them what to do when they have made
> converts in the neighbourhood too remote to be intimately
> attached to their own body, or in case people from a neighbour-

ing village came to them to learn the Christian faith. He should tell them first to make sure that the new converts are really converts to the faith of Christ and understand the *use* of the Creed, the Gospels, the Sacraments and the Ministry, and then to send word to the Bishop.

(*Spontaneous Expansion of the Church*)

Is this low church or high church doctrine? It seems to be both biblical and catholic and therefore to be the answer to our distresses. The difficulty is that we are faced with a church brought up in quite other ways, and a series of sects that have put that which the churches omitted or distorted into a heretical and schismatic framework. If we habitually treated the congregation as a church in the Pauline sense, and used the sacraments as if they were as important as we say they are, we should find that the problems begin to yield. The first of these prescriptions presupposes, of course, a revolution in foreign and professional attitudes; and this without doubt is where the missionary may make a start.

The sects (bodies originating mainly as protests against one or more of the churches, often starting as a revival movement within them, entirely national in leadership and finance, and always fundamentalist in theology) present a more complex problem. They are commonly more vital than the churches. They show a more lively initiative and develop a church life and cultus that is more satisfying — in ways good and less good — than that of the churches. They are of the land. Many China missionaries consider that they are the hope of the future. There are, however, items on the other side of the ledger. They are exceedingly fissiparous. Schism begets schism, and it also begets heresy, which is encouraged by nationalism. Rejecting the foreign church of the missionary and uninterested in his church history, they reject in effect the corporate fellowship in time and space of the Christians, and do not heed the lessons the fellowship has learned. So they are forced back on to "the Bible and the Bible alone the religion of Protestants." That is a false slogan: we may debate and differ upon the relations of Bible, church, and tradition; but we are bound to all three. The Bible alone, in artificial separation from the church, is in fact not sufficient. Church life compels elaboration, and that elaboration will be in a measure heretical. The particular heresies to which the church is drawn, in an era of nationalist sentiment, will be local. The African sects are frequently lax on polygamy, and some admit customs associated with witchcraft. Thus the sects can become the way back to paganism. Chinese fundamentalism is in its basic drives altogether too prone to feel about "salvation" as if it were the same sort of thing as the prosperity here and hereafter that is the goal of ordinary Chinese village religion; and this suggests that the Chinese sects are travelling the same road. All sects make much of the Holy Spirit and of the Second Coming. In this way they once again both protest against and supply a lack amongst ourselves, and in doing so fall into other not less dangerous error.

We must now turn somewhat rapidly to some of the particular aspects of the church work overseas; and, resisting the temptation to describe, confine ourselves as far as possible to positive suggestion.

Evangelism among the younger churches is more often the activity of the national than of the missionary, and of the layman rather than the professional. There is not half enough of it; but it is not so much exhortation to evangelize that is needed (for that, as we know in Britain, falls on largely deaf ears), as the habitual assumption that the church is an outward-looking, expansive body. As we should expect from our own experience, what is now called "the problem of communication" is the worst unsolved problem. There are very very few people in the churches who have thought through their faith in terms of the version of secularist socialist nationalism current in their surroundings; and the conversion of these lands will wait upon it. The first missionaries were often scholars; they learned the Chinese language, Chinese customs, Chinese philosophy, and Chinese history because without this understanding they could make no contact with their hearers. We have been softened by the prevalence and popularity of a semi-Christian Western culture and especially of the English language, and have allowed people to approach us and to become Christians, as it were, in the foreignized section of their minds. We are now paying for this. Serious grappling with the mind of China or India or anywhere else is a matter for the national. The foreign missionary can, however, serve as a useful work of reference as it were — if he knows his stuff. More missionaries would be of great value who had a good lay knowledge of Marxism, for example, or the philosophy of science, or Darwinism, or the sociology of knowledge, or the structure and social effects of the modern large-scale industrial enterprise.

The institutional work of the church overseas is of great complexity and variety because it has to be related to the real or assumed needs of the church and to the past, present, and future needs of the country and the plans of the civil authorities. It is at present falling between these several stools; the civil authorities are pressing for such things as greater and therefore much more expensive technical competence, while an increasing number of missionaries are restive about the declining religious quality. Present tendencies, if continued, will simply ensure that Christian institutions are second- or third-rate institutions.

It is likely that in any case the church will continue to control a large sector of education and medicine for only a short while. It is certain that an attempt to cut down the educational and medical work of the church, especially if it were imposed by the missions, would be bitterly resented by the whole body of the local Christian church, which is, for understandable reasons, passionately desirous of an increase of these services and less disposed than we are to ask questions about quality, and especially religious quality.

It seems to follow from the general theological presuppositions we have advanced about God as Creator and Redeemer, that education and medicine are both Christian concerns, whether or not religious education is included or an opportunity for evangelism provided. The three R's, like health, are things we desire, approve of, and should provide if adequate provision cannot yet be made by the community and we have the resources. The large bulk of our institutional work could well continue on that basis, as a genuine service to the community, but accepting much more willingly and whole-heartedly than at present the directions of the community, and not attempting to combine this social contribution with the main role of training in Christian faith and life. Experience in China suggests that it will be increasingly inportant, in any case, to put the main emphasis on Christian training in the congregation and in the home where it properly belongs. Once again, we must recover the proper truth of the church; in the slogan of the thirties: "Let the Church be the Church."

A most unsatisfactory tension in this and other matters is developing in Africa between missionaries who are deeply aware of the failings in the West of secular education, and African leaders who are more acutely conscious of Africa's need for precisely the Western skills that Western secular education, whatever its numerous shortcomings, does provide. This tension is not diminished by the fact that the experiences of other areas are mediated to Africa not directly, but through missionaries. (Few Chinese clergy have any considerable acquaintance with India or Africa, or vice versa.) Missionary evidence upon the lessons of other lands is probably suspect. What is required is direct cross-fertilization, and not only through London, Oxford, or New York.

This consideration leads on to some more general points about the critical importance of national Christian leadership. Although we are in many places much luckier than we deserve in the quantity and quality of the national leadership of the church, there is still far too little, and it is far too like ourselves. There is a general conviction that the first priority is the development of leadership, and a rather undefined hope that it may be genuinely national and bring into the *Una Sancta* the glories of the kingdom of the world. It is difficult to see how it can do so if it is mainly trained by us in our traditions. There is therefore a very strong case for the careful study of the sects. It is also desirable that young missionaries be trained, not by senior missionaries, but wherever possible — and it is much more possible than is usually realized — by nationals. When future national leaders are trained outside their own country, we should be much less concerned than we are to bring them up in the particular tradition which commends itself to us; and they should be invited to participate critically in such creative responses as may be found in our own church life to the challenge of the post-Christian proletarian west, instead of having a disproportionate amount of their time taken up with being Exhibit A at missionary meetings, a role which is generally extremely distasteful to them. It should also be realized that for reasons which are fairly evident, the hearts of many national Christian leaders are the scene of a warfare between gratitude, politeness, and resentment. Among us, it is the gratitude and the politeness that mainly present themselves, and the last is repressed; when the resentment comes out, it comes out with increased fury just because it has been so long repressed. This is to my mind the principal explanation of why Chinese Christians did not more defend their missionaries against attack. It is our business to create in the Christians from overseas whom we meet a sufficient confidence in us that they will speak the truth: they do not generally do so because they think we shall be offended. In this situation, training of nationals in this country can never have its full value.

It is, moreover, open to question whether training for Christian leadership, as distinguished from the acquisition of the technical skills that the worldwide dominance of Western scientific culture makes so essential, is always best acquired in this country at all. At all events, we should experiment much more than we do with such things as careful discussion with groups of national leaders and hardly any missionaries (and they genuinely sympathetic) whose purpose is to think of how a year or two in England can best be spent: the answers would assuredly differ from the sort of plans we usually make for them. Africans might learn more, in many cases, from time in India, than in England, and vice versa — but let their tours and their conferences be planned by Indians and Africans directly, with the role of the missionary confined (except where there is explicit invitation to do otherwise) to such matters as the making of initial contracts, arrangements of tickets and the like.

The drift of these remarks must now be clear: the missionary is not central; and where he is central, the effect is to distort the natural growth of the church. In China we have been demonstrated to be not only not central, but not even essential. The day of a similar demonstration in other lands may be nearer, and its coming more desirable, than we think; and it would be a pleasant change if that day were to be hastened by a true Christian response within the church rather than by pressure from outside — in prophetic terms, rather by the repentance of Israel than by the battering of Assyria.

These may seem utopian reflections in face of the immense measure of control and leadership still firmly in missionary hands. It was profoundly disconcerting to find in 1951 that so many of the same missionaries were still in control after Indian independence as were running things before it in 1944. The reasons will be found in Roland Allen's books and in some remarks, only apparently cynical, of a missionary friend writing from India in 1943: "I am coming to feel that this talk about training for freedom is a fraud. I may have been reading too much Dostoyevsky, but it seems to me that there are two things you can say about freedom. You don't get it until you fight for it; and when you do get it, it is full of unpleasant responsibilities and disappointment." In a situation in which Indians, for example, deeply resent the continued election of missionaries as bishops and yet go on electing them, what can the missionary do?

What would happen if all ordained missionaries in the churches of India, Pakistan, Burma, and Ceylon, or in the church of South India, or so many of them as can be persuaded to do so, would seek some suitable but early occasion of stating together that they will not allow their own names to go forward for episcopal election (in the improbable event of their being nominated) and will use such little influence as they may properly exert to prevent the election of fellow countrymen from their homelands? One man, or three, cannot do this without intolerable arrogance: the same objection would hardly apply to twenty or fifty.

What are the uses of missionaries? Indeed, are there any?

Let us consider first what advantages missionaries have, to set against their obvious disadvantage of lack of profound (sometimes lack even of superficial) knowledge of the people, the language, and the culture, and their dependence commonly on the maintenance of their own way of life.

First, they are heirs of a long Christian tradition. Dr. Timothy Tingfang Lew said once: "The trouble with these first-generation Christians is that they only see one thing." A man from a pagan background, who has become a Christian in his teens, commonly sees that which brought him to Christ with a clarity and depth that few of us can match; but he tends also to be one-eyed; and Dr. Lew, who was a third or fourth generation Christian, was himself not as comprehensive in his vision as he supposed. Missionaries are not necessarily more holy, more devout, more spiritual than Indian, Chinese, Japanese, or African Christians; but they are commonly more balanced, because the Christian faith is even today in our air and in our bones. We have acquired, without special study, some awareness of the long experience of the church, some knowledge of when and where this sort of problem, which has come up today in X, has been faced by the church before; whereas a national of the younger churches would be a man of exceptional wisdom and culture to have acquired the same knowledge.

Second, missionaries are in some respect more mobile, more disposable, and more free from local ties and social and family complications than nationals. This advantage — which must not be overstated, because these ties and complications are the stuff of which once redeemed, the Christian community must be built — is at present largely counterbalanced by our immersion in the maintenance of the duties taught by old occasions, the preservation of much ancient good. But this need not continue. Missionaries ought therefore to be specially useful as pioneers and experimenters. If they succeed, the church can enter into their heritage. If they fail, the church is not irretrievably harmed.

The role of missionaries is, then, an idea, ancillary. Not leaders — and not, please, trainers of leaders. It is our business, first, to belong to the church, and then to do such things as we are given to do by the church: even the pioneer in the geographical sense will not go forth without the commission of the church nearest to the area to which he goes. Indeed, the question, "What do missionaries do?" should not be raised until we have learned to "be." When we are in some sense disciplined to being part of the landscape, as much at home in Africa, India, or the South Seas as the color of our skin and the shape of our noses and the like permit, it will be time to start talking about doing.

This is a difficult lesson — full of frustrations for dynamic Westerners anxious to get on with the job and trained in a Christian tradition that is one-way and not two-way. We preach the gospel to others, and they listen. We open schools, and they learn. We are doctors, and they present their bodies for healing. We do good to people. Do we receive? A number of missionaries are uneasy about these things. We have been told by Asians that we must not be superior, and we strive not to be. But we are conscious that we give them things, and many of us cannot point with a similar certainty to what we have received. Father Kelly used to say that being ill in bed was the biggest test of Christian character that he knew, for it was a circumstance in which you can do little for others and are compelled to allow them to do things for you. Most of us do not meet such a challenge with grace; and this is because we have not grasped that charity, life in the Spirit, is not a one-way street, but a giving and a receiving. Does not this illuminate the anti-foreign feeling of younger churches, the clericalism and the anti-clericalism that are growing in England? If the intending missionary wants an aim in a phrase, let it be "to make friends," not of people "beloved in Christ" only, as by the man of whom his people observed mordantly, "He loves us only in the Lord," but friends *tout court,* like one's own college friends — and then be prepared also to be cut off from them, save in a spiritual sense, by events which neither we nor they can control.

If this is the aim, unrestricted fellowship with the people we deal with must be the first priority; and nothing can be tolerated that gets in its way. The pursuit of fellowship will take the modern missionary among many strange and revolutionary ways, as it took Charles Andrews in India. Yet this illustration may be misleading. The call of God will not necessarily be met by a rash of political missionaries. Charles Andrew and Michael Scott did not start in politics but in living with people, and the politics followed as an inevitable consequence of the circumstances of those people. What will follow for others will be declared in life with them and with God.

It may be politics. It may be the ordinary pastoral work in the countryside to which the ordained missionary, now being extruded from administration, may take a major contribution. It may be in Christian literature — if so, it will be by working alongside one or more nationals, for the age when we can be content with wooden translations or equally wooden "original" writing is past. It may be in *ashrams* and other experiments in Christian community. God will show us: but he can only declare his will to those who seek it — who accept his judgment and go out to meet him.

The "realignment" that is required of the individual is required also of the body. As the local state and the local church undertake to fall heir to the local functions of the mission, a residuary legatee has to be found also for the international functions of the mission. Among Anglicans an increasing sense of the Anglican communion as a body suggests that this will be the Archbishopric of Canterbury. Anglicans are, of course, well advised to remember that the Anglican communion is not one of the larger non-Roman communions, and that the pretentious claims on its behalf strike other people as ludicrous and offensive. But Anglicanism is where we Anglicans start, and not without temerity we may venture to suggest the lines upon which the ecumenical policy of the Patriarchate of Canterbury may be conducted. We use the word *Patriarchate* in recollection of the Pope's salutation to St. Anselm, and because Canterbury is regarded with affection and veneration by many outside as well as within the Anglican family of churches; and it is proper for us to concern ourselves with these matters because the policy adopted by Canterbury is not unrelated by any manner of means to the opinions, convictions, prejudices, and fears of Anglicans as a whole.

The worldwide diffusion of Anglican Christianity was, sociologically considered, a by-product of the *Pax Britannica*. With each year that passes, the social and political prestige of Anglicanism declines. At the same time, the pressure for unity in the younger churches will face us with more such dilemmas as already confront us in South India. Events in the younger churches will not be determined by what takes place in the vocations of Canterbury and York (which are divided) or the representative bodies of the Church of Ireland or the Episcopal Church in Scotland (which are likely to jump different ways). The younger churches will go as they believe God calls them. If, for example, the Church of England in two years' time takes a hostile or unbelieving attitude to what is now already silly to describe as the "South India experiment," that will not deter South India; but it will render her task of fidelity to Catholic order more difficult. An attitude which is defensive, which regards Catholic faith and order, ministry, and sacraments as treasures to be preserved from profane hands, will not help others to understand and desire them; and it will immensely reduce the ecumenical significance of Anglicanism. The only hope that Anglicanism can play the great part that the Lambeth Conferences have sketched is provided by Anglicanism's being ready to welcome the new united bodies that seek to grow in an understanding of the use of the things God has given us to preserve. The younger churches are surprisingly anxious for a maintenance of their ecumenical and international fellowships; but if this can only be had at the price of denying what seems to them the evident summons of God, they will sadly but unhesitatingly reject it. The tone of the Church of South India's reply to some Anglican questionings is indubitable on that score. For them it is a matter of "Whether it be right to serve God or man, judge ye."

The issue is that for us too. The argument so far has been in terms of ecclesiastical politics; for it is desirable that, if we are going to talk a good deal about preserving the Anglican heritage, we should know what that means in practical terms. But the serious considerations ought to be theological (although it is fair to say that in most of the historic schisms, as in those of today, sociological, national, cultural, psychological, personal, and all sorts of non-theological factors have played a dominant part). What, then, shall we think of our own heritage? Let us say crudely that Anglicanism is endangered today by those who in fear of Rome play down the Catholic elements that were not rejected at the Reformation. The Catholic episcopate, the Catholic priesthood, the Catholic sacraments are essential; and our distresses abroad and at home are in part due to our failure to value and use them properly. They are not an embarrassment, but a strength. Anglicanism is endangered by the attempt to fence these signs of the kingdom of Christ in the concrete and barbed wire of a theological system from which the Reformation delivered us. Roman theology is now more determinative for us than Roman practice; from both, as from those of other bodies, we have not a little to learn. Anglicanism is endangered by a superficially broad-minded distaste for theological and liturgical convictions. Anglicanism is finally endangered most of all by fear; and there are ominous signs that the theological and religious worlds are today frightened. If we tremble for the Ark of God, or for anything else, we shall surely go wrong. This is God's world, and let us go out into it to whatever he brings us. Let us use everything we have been given, not in the spirit of the man who wrapped his talent in a napkin, but in that of the man who went out and gained another ten.

These principles may set a course for Anglicans and for some others. If there is Canterbury, however, there are also Edinburgh, Geneva, Moscow, and Rome — but especially Geneva. If the renewed stress of recent years upon the study of the various rocks from which we have been hewn is not to change from a proper rededication to the things that God has given us to an obstinate settling into confessional air raid shelters, it must be balanced by a wider vision such as sustained the Bishops in 1948. This vision is focused for us in the World Council of Churches and the other ecumenical bodies. Let us not wax sentimental — or cynical. The World Council of Churches is not a church or a super-church or anything of that sort. You cannot be "in communion" with it, and it therefore lacks both the substance and the symbol of full unity. It is not "The Coming Great Church," but it points to it and is the way to it.

These are not, today, theologically fashionable observations. In this country especially, the ecumenical organizations are having a lean time. The idea of "reunion" advanced fast in the twenties on the wings of a theology that was relatively loose in its allegiance to churchly tradition. The impetus resulted in the formation of a number of organizations. Now that we have the structure, the theological tide seems to have swung away; and the bright young thinkers who were all for reunion thirty years ago are today investigating the byways of Calvin or Thomas, the Carolines, the Tractarians, John Owen, or Luther. The ecumenical bodies depend for influence on the quality of their leadership: on spiritual and intellectual depth, and on the clear demonstration that it is more effective to do things together than separately. It is widely felt that they are not giving leadership of this quality. It is less widely realized that this is a disaster. The hardening of denominational sentiment is not only a matter of the recovery of churchmanship. It is also a response of fear — a retreat from the ambiguities and complexities of the world, to what we know and love; a retreat from the present wrath of God, to his past mercies. Meanwhile, if the instructed Christian minority could not care more for its churchly life, the uninstructed majority of churchgoers, let alone the still larger majority who frequent us irregularly or not at all, could not care less. Once again, let us go out to meet God, even our God in judgment, terrible as a consuming fire.

Who then devised the torment? Love.
Love is the unfamiliar Name
Behind the hands that wove
The intolerable shirt of flame
Which human power cannot remove.
   We only live, only suspire
   Consumed by either fire or fire.

(T. S. Eliot, "Little Gidding")

This is one field for a living theology, a farsighted ecclesiastical statesmanship. Others have been referred to from time to time. Such a theology is badly needed. Anglo-Saxon mission policy, unlike that of German Protestants or Continental Roman Catholics, has been far too little directed by fundamental theological thinking: we have little "missiology." Roland Allen's books seem to have had little practical effect, perhaps because the administrative and psychological revolution they would entail was too great to be, as we say in our lazy, irreligious moments, "practical." So the theology was ignored. Today both the confessional revivals and the prevalence of biblical theology enable us to appreciate more readily the theological substructure of his thought. Even so, one would like to be sure that a newer biblical theology, and the experiences of the liturgical and evangelistic developments of continental Roman Catholics, were being studied as a matter of course by missionaries and especially in the training of missionaries. We need again to give earnest thought to the doctrines of the community and of the state; and with these, to the doctrines of work, of marriage, and of sex itself. Then further there is the whole question of the fostering of indigenous theologies.

The principal incentive to this, of course, will be the assumption of responsibility by nationals for the work of their own churches: that is the source of our Western theology. The process can be assisted, however, by missionaries who have digested their own theology thoroughly. Such men not only see it as a dogmatic system, but have a more sophisticated understanding of the contribution to it of the historical conditions under which it developed. They will be more sensitive to the significance of the culture of the country and of the secular trends, whether ancient or modern, local or worldwide, at work in the community.

The danger of all theological activity, of course, is that it is conceptual, and that *our* concepts are inescapably Western, mainly Latin and Greek. It is by no means evident that these are useful overseas. It may be that there will be no indigenous theology until the younger churches theologize from their experience, illuminated by the Bible, without going through the Greek and Latin developments. There are signs of this happening in China, of people theologizing from the Bible in the church. More fundamental is the need to develop the Christian imagination, which is deeper and more important than the Christian intelligence. Indeed, our own theology will only be completed when the Chinese, the Indian, the African, and the other Christian imaginations have been developed and have made their theological contributions explicit. "We without them shall not be made perfect," in Austin Farrer's phrase.

What shall we say by way of conclusion?

Charles Williams, who loved more than most the indwelling of Christ and his spirit in the members of his Body, which he called our "coinherence," has a fascinating passage in *The Descent of the Dove* in which he draws attention to the fact that in one year, 1534, Luther published the German translation of the Bible, Calvin composed the first draft of the *Institutes of the Christian Religion,* and Loyola and six companions took their vows. Elsewhere he remarks: "In England John Wesley, in South Italy Alphonsus Ligouri, pronounced with passion to the lowest classes . . . the Name of Salvation. . . . Had they ever met . . . they would not have approved of each other." Williams saw these "coincidences" as signs of the one activity of the Holy Ghost renewing our contrition, in one body if we will, across our divisions if we will not. This surely is how we should look at the immense range of missionaries — often mutually disapproving of each other's faith and works; of the Christians of the younger and the older churches with their wide variety of office, of belief, of hope, and of fear; and of the diverse responsibilities of the professional missionaries and those other Christians who serve their Lord as laymen. We do all belong together; as did Calvin and Luther and Loyola, More and Cranmer and Cartwright, Wesley and Ligouri and Joseph Butler; as do the men and women of our generation. And our hearts are not more torn than theirs. We belong together, not because our differences are unimportant, but because if there is anything that is true in us, it comes from the one source, the Holy Ghost.

We share one spirit, serve one mission, and expect one Lord. We have written critically of some of the ways that mission is now carried on: if we call for repentance, the call comes from the penitents' bench, and we have tried to free our words from the hyperbolic blackening of the past which commonly marks words from that source. A call to repentance is not a call to drop important work, but to do it otherwise. The mission of the church abides; and the times are short, in more senses than one.

Of those who may read this book, only a minority could consider working overseas, or indeed at home in some fresh, untried, financially imprudent venture. Even so, God calls more than hear. But the heart of the matter is not "Why not be a foreign missionary?" It is to try to find out quite freshly and without laying down conditions or making private reservations, what God desires of one. The particular vocation to the overseas part of the mission, as to the clerical or the monastic parts of the mission, comes to a few. But *all* of us without exception, by virtue of our calling as Christians, accept — or should accept, but widely do not — our work, our place, our family condition, as those to which God calls us.

There is an unreality about all this. Commonly, a pious minority make their decisions in conscious obedience to what they believe to be God's will. The rest of us pick our life's work or our life's partner for reasons good or bad, sensible or otherwise; but the choice is not consciously related to our position as friends of Christ. Commonly, "missions" are the concern of a pious minority — are not one of the expressions of the concern of the faithful for the evangelization of the world and the victory of the King, but a substitute for such a concern. As "religious" in the Roman world, so "missionaries" in the Protestant world have too often been regarded as the heroic saintly souls whose superabundant virtue will suffice to win salvation not only for themselves and their converts, but also for those who listen to their addresses and support them with funds. But Christ's death for us cannot become effective unless we allow him to work in us; and our obedience to God in his church cannot be carried on by proxy. The mission is entrusted to us all; our response to his trust is to find the place in it which God designs for us.

> Yet just as Christ has already fulfilled within Himself and pre-figured the salvation of the human race, likewise we in our turn can prefigure and prepare universal salvation by assuming inwardly through prayer the peoples that are still strangers to the Gospel so that there may even now exist though hidden this mystery of perfect praise that will be manifested at the end of time.
>
> (Daniélou, *The Salvation of the Nations*)

That is a task in which all Christians without exception can join — though it is not in fact always as easy as it looks "on paper." In what ways that prayer will lead us into the world to meet our Lord in his workings we may not know at all, and can never know with final completeness because there is always more to come. Nothing is more important than to know what appointment God has made for us; and no appointment is more worth keeping.

Bibliography of
David Macdonald Paton

1938/   *Reinhold Niebuhr, An Introduction to His Thought.* Lon-
1939   don: Student Christian Movement.

1939   *Blind Guides.* London: SCM Press.

1944   "Christian Work in Chinese Government Universities."
        In *International Review of Mission*, 33.

1946   *Religion in the University.* London: SCM Press.

1947   "The Mission of the Christian University." In *Inter-
        national Review of Missions*, 36.

1949   *FUTC* (Foochow Union Theological College). London:
        CMS.

1950   "Theological Training in China." In *East and West*
        (1950).

1951   "First Thoughts on the Debacle of Christian Missions in
        China." In *International Review of Mission*, 40. (Writ-
        ten as "A China Missionary").

1953   *Christian Missions and the Judgment of God.* London:
        SCM Press.

1957   With J. T. Martin. *Paragraphs for Sundays and Holidays.*
London: SCM Press.
"Church Life in China Today." In *Christian Century* (24
July).

1958   *Essays in Anglican Self-Criticism.* (Ed. with Introduc-
tion.) London: SCM Press.
"The Question of Authority." In *Christ Our Passover —
The Liturgical Observance of Holy Week,* edited by J. T.
Martin. London: SCM Press.
Church and Race in South Africa. (Ed.) London: SCM
Press.

1959   "The Church in the World: The Uitlander in No Man's
Land." In *The Missionary Church in East and West.*
(Ed. with C. C. West.) London: SCM Press.

1960   *The Ministry of the Spirit — Selected Writings of Roland
Allen.* (Ed.) London: World Dominion Press.
Chapter in *No Pious Person,* edited by George Every.
London: Faith Press.
"The Relevance of Roland Allen." In *Part-time Priests,*
edited by Robin Denniston. London: Skeffington.
"Three Prophets: F. D. Maurice, H. H. Kelly, Roland
Allen." In *Frontier* (August 1960).
"Theological Training in the Younger Churches" (re-
view). In *East and West Review* (October 1960).

1961   "Preface to British Edition." In *The Old and New in the
Church — World Council of Churches Commission on
Faith and Order Report.* London: SCM Press.

1962   *Anglicans and Unity.* London: A. R. Mowbray and Co.
"The Third Assembly — Some Critical Observations."
In *Ecumenical Review* (January 1962).
*The Parish Communion Today — The Report of the 1962
Conference of Parish and People.* (Ed.) London: SPCK.

1963   *Mission and Communication — The Report of the 1963
Conference of Parish and People.* (Ed.) London: SPCK.

1964   *One Church Renewed for Mission.* London: SCM Press. "La Communion anglicane et le mouvement oecumenique." In *Rythmes du Mondes* (1964), no. 2.

1965   *New Forms of Ministry.* (Ed. with Introduction.) London: Edinburgh House Press.
With R. M. C. Jeffery. *Christian Unity and the Anglican Communion.* London: Church Information Office. (Revised edition, 1966.)

1966   *The Anglican Communion and Latin America* (report of a consultation). London: SPCK. (No author given, report drafted by Paton.)

1967   With R. Lathom. *Point of Decision.* London: SPCK/Epworth Press.

1968   "Roland Allen — A Biographical and Theological Essay." In *Reform of the Ministry: A Study in the Work of Roland Allen.* (Ed.) London: Lutterworth Press.
Anglikanerna och Kyrkornas varldsrad (Anglicans and the World Council of Churches). In *Credo*, Uppsala.

1969   "Secular Ecumenism and the Anglican Future." In *Modern Churchman* (April 1969).
"The Positive Idea of a Wider Episcopal Fellowship." In *Lambeth Essays on Unity*, edited by the Archbishop of Canterbury, London: SPCK; and in *Lambeth Conference 1968 Preparatory Essays*, London, SPCK.
Foreword to *The Unity Book of Prayers.* London: Geoffrey Chapman.

1975   "Nairobi, 1975 — A Personal Account." In *Breaking Barriers, Nairobi 1975, The Official Report of the Fifth Assembly of the World Council of Churches.* (Ed.) London: SPCK and Grand Rapids: Wm. B. Eerdmans.

1978   "Chinese Deaconess." In *Theology* (July 1978).

1983   Edited with C. H. Long. *The Compulsion of the Spirit — A Roland Allen Reader.* Grand Rapids: Wm. B. Eerdmans; Cincinnati, Ohio: Forward Movement Publications.

"Twelve Assumptions about Confessing the Faith in the Global Village." In *New Fire* 7 (Winter 1983). (Also in *East Asia Journal of Theology* 2, no. 2 [1984].)

1984   Keynote Address to Pacific Basin Conference on Roland Allen. In *Setting Free the Ministry of the People of God,* edited by G. Davies. Cincinnati, Ohio: Forward Movement Publications.

1985   *RO — The Life and Times of Bishop Hall of Hong Kong.* Hong Kong: The Diocese of Hong Kong and Macao.

1989   Foreword to A. Talltort, *Sacrament and Growth: A Study of the Sacramental Dimension of Expansion in the Life of the Local Church, as Reflected in the Theology of Roland Allen.* Uppsala.

1990   "China: Some Things to Think About." In *Weight of Glory,* edited by Hardy and Sedgwick. University of Hull.

NOTE: This list excludes Paton's many book reviews and some of his articles published in *The Church Times, Theology,* and *Frontier,* written over a period of thirty years.

The bulk of his papers and correspondence is deposited in the archives of Selly Oak Colleges in Birmingham alongside his father's papers. There are much smaller deposits in the USPG archive at Partnership House and in the Lambeth Palace Library. A few of his papers remain in the present writer's possession.

David M. M. Paton

Further Reading

Paton was much influenced in his theology by Jean Daniélou's *The Salvation of the Nations* (Sheed and Ward, 1949); by Max Warren's *The Christian Mission* (SCM Press, 1951), *The Truth of Vision* (Canterbury Press, 1948), and *The Calling of God* (Lutterworth, 1944); by his father William Paton's work, especially *The White Man's Burden* (Epworth Press, 1939); by Reinhold Niebuhr's *Moral Man and Immoral Society* (Scribner, 1933); and by F. D. Maurice's *The Kingdom of Christ* (Allenson, 1959). The books on Communism and modern Chinese history to which he made reference are now superseded, not least by the events of the last five years; of these the most important was C. P. Fitzgerald's *Revolution in China* (Cresset Press, 1952). Roland Allen's work on mission remained an inspiration (he edited two selections of Allen's writings — see bibliography), especially *Missionary Methods: St. Paul's or Ours* (World Dominion Press, 1930), and *Spontaneous Expansion of the Church* (World Dominion Press, 1949), as did the writings and personality of Bishop R. O. Hall, *The Art of the Missionary* (SCM Press, 1942 — see also Paton's life of Hall). For developments on India, he was influenced by Bishop Lesslie Newbigin, *A South India Diary* (SCM Press, 1951) and *The Re-union of the Church* (SCM Press, 1948). Austin Farrer's books informed some of the discussion in the last chapter: *The Glass of Vision* (Dacre Press, 1948), *A Rebirth of Images* (Dacre Press, 1949), and *A Study in St. Mark* (Dacre Press, 1951).

113

Of contemporary books dealing with the church in China, some important works are Zhao Fusan (Chao Fu San), "The Penitence and Renewal of the Church in China," in *Essays in Anglican Self-Criticism* (ed. Paton, SCM Press, 1958); George Hood, *Neither Bang nor Whimper: The End of a Missionary Era in China* (Singapore, 1991); Alan Hunter and Kim-Kwong Chan, *Protestantism in Contemporary China* (Cambridge, 1993); Donald E. Macinnis, *Religion in China Today, Policy and Practice* (Orbis, 1989); Edmond Tang and Jean-Paul Wiest, *The Catholic Church in Modern China* (Orbis, 1993); K. H. Ting, *Christianity with a Chinese Face* (Forward Movement Publications, 1985); Bob Whyte, *Unfinished Encounter: China and Christianity* (Collins, 1988); and Philip Wickeri, *Seeking the Common Ground: Protestant Christianity, the Three Self Movement and China's United Front* (Orbis, 1988).